Tucholsky Wagner Zola Scott Sydow Freud Schlegel
Turgenev Fonatne Wallace
Twain Walther von der Vogelweide Fouqué Friedrich II. von Preußen
Weber Freiligrath Frey
Fechner Fichte Weiße Rose von Fallersleben Kant Ernst Frommel
Richthofen
Hölderlin
Engels Fielding Eichendorff Tacitus Dumas
Fehrs Faber Flaubert
Maximilian I. von Habsburg Fock Eliasberg Zweig Ebner Eschenbach
Feuerbach Eliot Vergil
Ewald
Goethe Elisabeth von Österreich London
Mendelssohn Balzac Shakespeare Dostojewski Ganghofer
Lichtenberg Rathenau Doyle Gjellerup
Trackl Stevenson Tolstoi Hambruch
Mommsen Lenz Droste-Hülshoff
Thoma Hanrieder
Dach von Arnim Hägele Hauff Humboldt
Verne
Reuter Rousseau Hagen Hauptmann Gautier
Karrillon Garschin
Defoe Hebbel Baudelaire
Damaschke Descartes
Hegel Kussmaul Herder
Wolfram von Eschenbach Dickens Schopenhauer Rilke George
Darwin Melville Grimm Jerome
Bronner Bebel Proust
Campe Horváth Aristoteles
Bismarck Vigny Barlach Voltaire Federer Herodot
Gengenbach Heine
Storm Casanova Tersteegen Grillparzer Georgy
Chamberlain Lessing Langbein Gilm Gryphius
Brentano Lafontaine
Strachwitz Claudius Schiller Kralik Iffland Sokrates
Bellamy Schilling
Katharina II. von Rußland Gerstäcker Raabe Gibbon Tschechow
Löns Hesse Hoffmann Gogol Wilde Vulpius
Luther Heym Hofmannsthal Gleim
Roth Klee Hölty Morgenstern
Heyse Klopstock Kleist Goedicke
Luxemburg Puschkin Homer Mörike
La Roche Horaz Musil
Machiavelli Kierkegaard Kraft Kraus
Navarra Aurel Musset
Nestroy Marie de France Lamprecht Kind Kirchhoff Hugo Moltke
Laotse Ipsen Liebknecht
Nietzsche Nansen
Marx Ringelnatz
von Ossietzky Lassalle Gorki Klett Leibniz
May vom Stein Lawrence Irving
Petalozzi Knigge
Platon Pückler Michelangelo Kafka
Sachs Poe Kock
Liebermann Korolenko
de Sade Praetorius Mistral Zetkin

The publishing house tredition has created the series **TREDITION CLASSICS**. It contains classical literature works from over two thousand years. Most of these titles have been out of print and off the bookstore shelves for decades.

The book series is intended to preserve the cultural legacy and to promote the timeless works of classical literature. As a reader of a **TREDITION CLASSICS** book, the reader supports the mission to save many of the amazing works of world literature from oblivion.

The symbol of **TREDITION CLASSICS** is Johannes Gutenberg (1400 – 1468), the inventor of movable type printing.

With the series, tredition intends to make thousands of international literature classics available in printed format again – worldwide.

All books are available at book retailers worldwide in paperback and in hardcover. For more information please visit: www.tredition.com

tredition was established in 2006 by Sandra Latusseck and Soenke Schulz. Based in Hamburg, Germany, tredition offers publishing solutions to authors and publishing houses, combined with worldwide distribution of printed and digital book content. tredition is uniquely positioned to enable authors and publishing houses to create books on their own terms and without conventional manufacturing risks.

For more information please visit: www.tredition.com

# Half Hours in Bible Lands, Volume 2 Patriarchs, Kings, and Kingdoms

P. C. (Phineas Camp) Headley

# Imprint

This book is part of the TREDITION CLASSICS series.

Author: P. C. (Phineas Camp) Headley
Cover design: toepferschumann, Berlin (Germany)

Publisher: tredition GmbH, Hamburg (Germany)
ISBN: 978-3-8491-5410-3

www.tredition.com
www.tredition.de

Isaac and Esau

Job and His Three Friends.

THE BIBLE AND THE HOLY LAND.

PATRIARCHS, KINGS, AND KINGDOMS.


SCENES IN THE LIVES OF THE PATRIARCHS.


The patriarchs might be called family kings--the divinely appointed
rulers of households. They were the earliest sovereigns under God of
which we have any account. Their authority was gradually extended by
the
union of households, whose retinue of servants was often large, and
their wealth very great. The founder and leader of the patriarchal line
chosen by God from the wealthy nomades, or wandering farmers of the
fruitful valleys, was Abram. A worshipper of the Infinite One, he
married Sarai, a maiden of elevated piety and personal beauty. And
doubtless they often walked forth together beneath the nightly sky,
whose transparent air in that latitude made the stars impressively--

"The burning blazonry of God!"

Upon the hill-tops around, were the observatories and altars of Chalde-
an
philosophy, whose disciples worshipped the host of Heaven. In the
serenity of such an hour, with the white tents reposing in the distance,
and the "soul-like sound" of the rustling forest alone breaking the
stillness, it would not be strange, as they gazed on flaming Orion and
the Pleiades, if they had bowed with the Devotee of Light, while--

  "Beneath his blue and beaming sky,
   He worshipped at their lofty shrine,
   And deemed he saw with gifted eye,
   The Godhead in his works divine."

But a purer illumination than streamed from that radiant dome,
brought
near in his majesty the Eternal, and like the holy worshippers of Eden,
they adored with subdued and reverent hearts, their infinite Father.

There is great sublimity and wonderful power in the purity and growth

of
religious principle, in circumstances opposed to its manifestation. The
temptations resisted--the earnest communion with each other--the
glorious aspirations and soarings of imagination, when morning broke
upon the summits, and evening came down with its stars, and its rising
moon, flooding with glory nature in her repose. These, and a thousand
lovely and touching scenes of that pastoral life, are all unrecorded.
The great events in history, and bold points in character, are seized by
the inspired penman as sufficient to mark the grand outline of God's
providential and moral government over the world, and his care of his
people.

Just when it would best accomplish his designs, which are ever march-
ing
to their fulfillment, Jehovah called to Abram, and bade him go to a
distant land which he would show him. With his father-in-law, and
with
Lot, his flocks and herds, he journeyed toward Palestine. When he
arrived at Haran, in Mesopotamia, pleased with the country, and probably
influenced by the declining health of the aged Terah, he took up his
residence there. Here he remained till the venerable patriarch, Sarai's
father, died. The circle of relatives bore him to the grave, and kept
the days of mourning. But the dutiful daughter wept in the solitary
grief of an orphan's heart. A few years before she had lost a brother,
and now the father to whom she was the last flower that bloomed on
the
desert of age, and who lavished his love upon her, was buried among
strangers.

Then the command to move forward to his promised inheritance came
again
to Abram. With Sarai he journeyed on among the hills, encamping at
night
beside a mountain spring, and beneath the unclouded heavens arching
their path, changeless and watchful as the love of God--exiles by the
power of their simple faith in him. Soon as they reached Palestine,
Abram consecrated its very soil by erecting a family altar, first in the
plain of Moreh, and again on the summits that catch the smile of morning
near the hamlet of Bethel.

Months stepped away, rapidly as silently, old associations wore off, and Abram was a wealthy and happy man in the luxuriant vales of Canaan. His
flocks dotted the plains, and his cattle sent down their lowing from encircling hills. But more than these to him was the affection of his beautiful wife. Her eye watched his form along the winding way, when with the ascending sun he went out on the dewy slopes, and kindled with
a serene welcome when at night-fall he returned for repose amid the sacred joys of home.

At length there came on a fearful famine. The rain was withholden, and the dew shed its benediction no more upon the earth. He was compelled to
seek bread at the court of Pharaoh, or perish. Knowing the power of female beauty, and the want of principle among the Egyptian princes, he
was afraid of assassination and the captivity of Sarai which would follow. Haunted with this fear, he told her to say that she was his sister--which was not a direct falsehood, but only so by implication. According to the Jewish mode of reckoning relationship, she might be called a sister; and Abram stooped to this prevarication under that terrible dread which, in the case of Peter, drove a true disciple of Christ to the brink of apostacy and despair.

Results of Prevarication. Peter denying his Master.

But his deception involved him in the very difficulty he designed to escape. The king's courtiers saw the handsome Hebrew, and extolled her
beauty before him. He summoned her to the apartments of the palace, and
captivated by her loveliness, determined to make her his bride. During the agonizing suspense of Abram, and the concealed anguish of Sarai in her conscious degradation, the hours wore heavily away, until the judgment of God upon the royal household brought deliverance. Pharaoh,
though an idolater, knew by this supernatural infliction, that there was guilt in the transaction, and called Abram to an account. He had nothing
to say in self-acquittal, and with a strange magnanimity, was sent away quietly, with his wife and property, followed only by the reproaches of Pharaoh, and his own wakeful conscience.

Abram returned to Palestine, became a victor in fierce battles with a vastly outnumbering foe, and was in possession of a splendid fortune.

Whether in Egypt, or in his tent on the plains of Palestine, Abram, with

12

all the patriarchs, was a true gentleman. We may doubt whether any
modern school of refinement in manners could furnish any nobler ex-
amples
of dignity and civility in personal learning and manners, than were the
rich dwellers in ancient Palestine. Subjects fell prostrate before
sovereigns; equals, when they met, inclined the head toward the breast,
and placed the right hand on the left breast. Of the Great King it is
written, "Come, let us bow down; let us worship before the Lord our
Maker."

Jehovah appeared to Abram in a glorious vision, talking with him as
friend to friend. He fell on his face in the dust, as did the exile of
Patmos ages after, while a voice of affection and hope carne from the
bending sky: "I am the Almighty God; walk before me and be thou
perfect." The solemn covenant involving the greatness and splendor of
the people and commonwealth that should spring from the solitary
pair,
was renewed; and as an outward seal, he was named Abraham, The
father of
a great multitude--and his wife Sarah, The princess. Still he laughed at
the absurdity that Sarah would ever be a mother, and invoked a blessing
on Ishmael, but evidently said nothing to her upon a subject dismissed
as incredible from his thoughts. For when the celestial messengers were
in the tent, on their way to warn Lot, she listened to their earnest
conversation, conccaled by the curtains, and hearing that repeated
promise based on the immutability of God, also laughed with bitter
mirth
at her hopeless prospect in regard to the marvelous prediction. And
when
one of the Angels, who was Jehovah veiled in human form, as afterward
"manifest in the flesh," charged her with this unbelief and levity, the
discovery roused her fears, and approaching him, without hesitation,
she
denied the fact. He knew perfectly her sudden apprehension, and only
repeated the accusation, enforced by a glance of omniscience, like that
which pierced the heart of Peter.

The group separated, and two of those bright beings went to Sodom.
The

next morning Abraham walked out upon the plain, and looked toward the
home of Lot. He saw the smoke as of a great furnace going up to the calm
azure, from the scathed and blackened plains, where life was so busy and
joyous a few hours before! With a heavy heart he returned to his tent,
arid brought Sarah forth to behold the scene. She clung with trembling
to his side, while she listened to the narration of the terrible
overthrow of those gorgeous cities, and the rescue of her brother's
household, and beheld in the distance the seething and silent grave of
millions, sending up a swaying column of ebon cloud, like incense, to
God's burning indignation against sin.

They left the vale of Mamre, and journeyed to Gera, where, with a
marvellous forgetfulness of the past, the beauty of Sarah again led them
into deception and falsehood, and with the same result as before.
Abimelech, the king, would have taken her for his wife as Abraham's
sister, had not God appeared in a dream, threatening immediate death.
Upon pleading his innocence, he was spared, and expostulating with his
guest, generously offered him a choice of residence in the land; but
rebuked Sarah with merited severity.

Prophecy and covenant now hastened to their fulfillment. Sarah gave
birth to a son, and with the name of God upon her lips, she gave
utterance to holy rapture. With all her faults, she was a pious and
noble woman. She meant to train him for the Lord, and therefore when she
saw young Ishmael mocking at the festival of his weaning, she be-
sought
her husband to send away the irreverent son, whose influence might ruin
the consecrated Isaac. Hagar, with a generous provision for her wants,
was a fugitive; and the Most High approved the solicitude of a mother
for an only child, around whose destiny was gathered the interest of
ages, and the hopes of a world.

And now, with the solemn shadows of life's evening hours falling around
her, and a heart subdued by the discipline of Providence, in the fulness

of love which had been rising so long within the barriers of hope deferred, she bent prayerfully over the very slumbers of that fair boy, and taught him the precious name of God with the first prattle of his infant lips. How proudly she watched the unfolding of this bud of promise! When, in the pastimes of childhood, he played before the tent door, or, with a shout of gladness, ran to meet Abraham returning from the folds, her calm and glowing eye marked his footsteps, and her grateful aspirations for a blessing on the lad, went up to the Heaven of heavens. At length he stood before her in the manliness and beauty of youth, unscarred by the rage of passions, and with a brow open and laughing as the radiant sky of his own lovely Palestine.

Hagar in the Wilderness.

It was a morning which flooded the dewy plains with glory, and filled the groves with music, when Abraham came in from his wonted com-munion
with God, and called for Isaac, and told him to prepare for a three days' journey in the wilderness. How tenderly was Sarah regarded in this

scene of trial! Evidently no information of the awful command to sacrifice the son of her old age was made to her. She might have read something fearful in the lines of anxious thought and the workings of deep emotion in the face of Abraham. But he evaded all inquiries on the subject, "clave the wood," and accompanied by two of his young men, turned from his dwelling with a blessing from that wondering mother, and

was soon lost from her straining vision among the distant hills. Upon the third day he saw the top of Mount Moriah kindling in the rising sun,

and taking Isaac alone, ascended to the summit, whereon was to be reared

an altar, which awakened more intense solicitude in heaven, than any offering before or since, except on Calvary, where God's "only be-gotten and well-beloved Son" was slain. There is no higher moral sublimity than

the unwavering trust and cheerful obedience of this patriarch, when the very oath of the Almighty seemed perjured, and the bow of promise blotted from the firmament of faith!

But he believed Jehovah, and would have clung to his assurance, though

the earth had reeled in her orbit, and every star drifted from its moorings. He prayed for strength, with his hand on the forehead of his submissive son.

"He rose up, and laid
The wood upon the altar. All was done,
He stood a moment--and a deep, quick flush
Passed o'er his countenance; and then he nerved
His spirit with a bitter strength, and spoke--
'Isaac! my only son'--the boy looked up,
And Abraham turned his face away, and wept.
'Where is the lamb, my father?' O, the tones,
The sweet, the thrilling music of a child!
How it doth agonize at such an hour!
It was the last, deep struggle--Abraham held
His loved, his beautiful, his only son,
And lifted up his arm, and called on God
And lo! God's angel staid him--and he fell
Upon his face and wept."

The years fled, the good old Abraham died, and Isaac succeeded him to the patriarchal honors. He had two sons, Esau and Jacob. The elder brother was irreligious, and married a heathen wife. God had rejected him, and promised to Jacob the birthright; in other words, he was to be the chief patriarch, through whose descendants the Messiah should come.
He was his mother's favorite boy, while Isaac clung to Esau.

When the fond father became weak and blind from age, feeling that death
was near, one day he called Esau, and told him as he might die sudden-ly,
to get him venison, and prepare for the solemn occasion of receiving his parting blessing, which should secure the privileges and pre-eminence of
the first-born. The hunter went into the fields, and Rebekah recollected that Jacob had purchased the birthright of his brother for a mess of pottage one day when he came in from the chase faint with hunger and exhaustion. She determined by a stroke of management to secure the patriarchal benediction. She sent him to the flocks after two kids, which were prepared with the savory delicacy his father loved, dressed him up in Esau's apparel, covering his hands and neck to imitate the hairiness of the rightful heir, and sent him to the beside of the dying Isaac. When the patriarch inquired who he was, he replied, "I am Esau, thy first-born." This was beyond belief, because even the skillful hunter could scarcely, without a miracle, so soon bring in the game, and dress it for his table. Jacob was called to his side, and he felt of his hands; the disguise completed the delusion, although his voice had the milder tone of the young shepherd to that father's ear. He repeated the interrogation concerning his name, then embracing him, pronounced in a
strain of true poetry, the perpetual blessing of Jehovah's favor upon his undertakings, and his posterity. The stratagem had succeeded, and Jacob hastened to inform his mother of the victory, just as Esau entered. When Isaac discovered the mistake, he trembled with excite-ment,
while his son cried in anguish, "Bless even me also, O my father!" That cry pierced the breaking heart of the aged man, but it was a fruitless lament, He was inflexible, and Esau wept aloud over his blasted hopes; plotting at the same time, in his awakened enmity, the murder of Jacob.

This scene of deception, disappointment, and providential working, the introductory picture brings vividly before us.

The patriarchs were generally shepherds, and when we read in the Bible
of shepherds, we have but a poor impression of their business, if we think only of the keeping of the small flocks kept in the fenced fields and yards of modern farmers. They made their wealth chiefly by feeding
immense flocks and herds. They had extensive open plains; and were obliged to watch the animals to prevent their being lost, stolen by robbers, or devoured by ferocious beasts. When it was at all safe, the shepherds and their flocks slept in the fields, beneath the open sky, or under the sheltering trees.

The Welcome to a Wayward Son.

If the country was infested by dangerous men or animals, the owners of the flocks built the fold or sheep-cote. This enclosure was sometimes merely a rude pen. The walls were of wood or stone, with a thatched roof--if they had any at all. The shepherd follows a wayward sheep, and brings him back to a place of safety.

Thus the Good Shepherd of souls, whose disciples, like the flocks of the East, "know his voice," with his rod of affliction restrains the wandering and keeps securely the trusting ones.

Occasionally a rich land owner would make an expensive fold--a kind of
town or fortress for his flocks. Keeping the sheep in the air, it was believed improved the texture of the wool, making it softer and firmer than when exposed to the sweating and vapors which would necessari-
ly
result from crowding them often and long into enclosures.

Abraham, Isaac, and Jacob, were among the richest shepherds of antiquity, and stand alone in moral grandeur of character, so far as we have any records of the Hebrew husbandmen.

The great enemy of the sheep the world over, is the wolf--a cunning, savage, and daring creature. A lamb of the flock seems to be a dainty feast for him. He relishes even a child; the human delicacy is quite as delicious as the other. A mother, with three children, was once riding in a sledge in a desolate region, when a pack of wolves came running after her. She drove rapidly on, but they came nearer and nearer, until their hot breath fell on her face. In her terror, she threw one of the children to the hungry wolves, hoping thus to pacify or check them until
she could get out of their reach. Soon, however, they came galloping on, surrounding her sledge, and she flung another upon the snow. A brief delay, and they were once more around her, and the last child was given
to the beasts; and then she reached her home in safety.

When she told the story to her neighbors, an exasperated peasant hewed
her down with an axe, because she fed the wolves on her own offspring, selfishly saving by the sacrifice, her own life.

How like the destroyers of human virtue, and the great destroyer

himself! Wolves in sheep's clothing, stealing upon unguarded victims,
and glorying in the destruction of all that is "lovely and of good
report." for the transitory present and endless future!

We now turn to the annals of a patriarchal life which is entirely new,
and intensely interesting--the only record of the kind in the Bible.

The inspired history introduces him in the following words: "There was
a
man in the land of Uz, whose name was Job." This region was in Eastern
Arabia, and probably near the home of Abram when he was summoned
by God
to leave his idolatrous friends and neighbors in "Ur of the Chaldees."

It is thought he lived not far from the time of the great founder of the
Hebrew patriarchy. Job was probably a descendant of Nahor, Abram's
brother. He was a devout, rich, and benevolent Gentile patriarch. The
princely fortune of this "greatest of all the men of the East," is
indicated by an inventory of his flocks and herds. He had "seven
thousand sheep, and three thousand camels, and five hundred yoke of
oxen, and five hundred she asses." His household was also "very great."
This mighty man was a humble servant of God; and Satan could not
bear to
see his influence and prosperity; and he determined to make him the
shining mark of his enmity to God and man.

The mysterious account of his entrance upon the cruel work of attempt-
ed
ruin, is in the following words: "Now there was a day when the sons of
God came to present themselves before the Lord, and Satan came also
among them." The saints of that early age were called "Sons of God,"
but
the meaning seems to be that either Satan was permitted to appear in a
gathering of angels who, returning from their ministries of love, were
reporting to their king, and awaiting new instructions, or, it is
designed only to represent the real character and power of the tempter,
in contrast with the loyalty of God's servant.

The whole narrative bears the marks of a real history; and Jehovah is
not limited by our ideas of what he can consistently do. "My ways are

not your ways, nor my thoughts your thoughts, saith the Lord."

The devil charged Job with selfish motives in serving God. He could afford to be religious with such rare and splendid prosperity. To show to the universe Satan's lying malice, his loyal subject's holy character, and to comfort his people in all the ages following, while the discipline purified and beautified the sufferer, he told the adversary to try the patriarch with a change of circumstances--the severest trials; only his body must not be touched.

The gratified fiend hastened away to his attack upon the unsuspecting friend of God, over whom he anticipated a great victory. The patriarch's family was large, and evidently a united and happy one. They had their anniversary festivals, which were hallowed by religious services; the faithful and affectionate father offering sacrifices on such occasions. The Lord was recognized amid the most joyful scenes of social life; and not, as in many prosperous households of Christian name in all the ages since, excluded from the circle of pleasure like an unwelcome, unworthy
guest.

The Cruel Husbandman.

The birthday seems to have been the favorite anniversary; and at the
very moment Satan left Jehovah, the children were assembled at the
house
of the oldest brother. Job was not there. He may have gone away for
awhile, or not yet have joined the rejoicing company.

For a messenger rushed into his presence with the startling intelligence
that the lawless Sabeans living in the region, had fallen upon the
servants keeping the oxen and asses, and slaying them, had taken the
animals away. No sooner had the devil obtained permission to engage,
in
the wicked enterprise, than he found ready agents among men. And
before
the evil report was finished, another terrified, excited servant, came
in, saying that the lightning of heaven had consumed the seven thousand
sheep.

This intelligence was falling from the lips of the only shepherd who
escaped the devouring fire, when a third messenger entered, pale with
alarm, and announced the raid of three companies of Chaldeans upon
the
keepers of the three thousand camels, killing all but the bearer of the
news, and driving off the beasts of burden. The trembling man was
interrupted by the sudden appearance of the fourth servant, wild with
terror, crowning the crushing tidings already received, by telling Job
that a gale from the wilderness had swept down upon the eldest son's
dwelling, where the whole family were, excepting the patriarch, and
thrown walls and roof into a common wreck, burying his ten children
under the fragments.

We cannot easily imagine the stunning effect of these reports, following
each other like successive claps of thunder from a cloudless sky. Satan
was watching the effect, ready to exult over the first expression of
repining and rebellion. But how sublime the resignation of the loyal
heart of the childless, homeless, and penniless sufferer! After the
eastern custom in time of affliction, he cut off his hair, rent his
robe, fell upon the ground, and worshipped. The lips, tremulous with
sorrow, uttered the often-quoted and beautiful words: "The Lord gave,

and the Lord hath taken away; blessed be the name of the Lord." No
disloyal act, or foolish complaint against Jehovah, gratified the
expectant enemy of God and man. But Satan was not satisfied with the
trial of faith. He was allowed to appear before God, and in answer to
the questioning respecting the patriarch's lofty yet meek submission,
basely and meanly declared that if he had been permitted to torture the
body, he should have succeeded in proving Job to be a hypocrite. The
Lord had purposed to silence the devil, and thoroughly try and sanctify
his own child. So he told the tempter to do what he pleased, only he
must spare life.

Suddenly poor Job was covered with burning ulcers, which defiled his
form until he scraped it with a piece of broken pitcher. While sitting
in the dust, a wretched mass of corruption, he found a new tempter in
the person of his wife: She asked him if he could still "retain his
integrity," and urged him to "curse God and die." Beautifully again his
breaking heart uttered its loyalty. Charging her with folly, he
inquired: "What! shall we receive good at the hand of God, and shall we
not receive evil?"

The scene of sorrow is now changed. Job had three friends living in the
country not far off, who were clearly intelligent, noble men. They heard
of his calamities, and started on a visit of condolence. When they came
in sight of him, he was so changed that at first they did not know him.
They wept aloud, rent their robes, and scattered dust on their heads, to
express their overwhelming grief. There he sat, in miserable poverty
and
disease, and all around him the ruins of his just before magnificent
fortune, and the bodies or graves of his sons and daughters. They
approached him, and could say nothing, but sat down with him seven
days
and nights without speaking a word--an awful, expressive silence. At
length Job could refrain no longer, but in his despondency, began to
bewail his birth, and wish he had at least died in earliest infancy.
Then was opened a long, eloquent, and wonderful discussion by the
mourning company upon the providence and grace of God.

Jehovah at length spake from the rolling cloud, borne on the "wings of
the wind," and indicated his dealings with a fallen race, pointing the
debaters for illustrations of power, wisdom, and glory, to his works of
creation, from the "crooked serpent" to "Orion and the Pleiades,"

floating in the nightly sky--the wonders of ocean, earth, and air.

Among the animals to which reference is made, there are three
conspicuous ones, about which naturalists disagree--they cannot
certainly tell us what they were. These are the unicorn, supposed by
many to be the rhinoceros of the present day; the behemoth, thought to
be the hippopotamus or river-horse; and the leviathan, which answers
very well to the whale.

The description of the war horse is the finest ever written, and given
in a few words; and yet he had not been seen amid the wildest storm of
battle, bearing his rider to the flaming mouths of ordnance, and through
the leaden hail of numberless infantry arms. "Hast thou given the horse
strength? hast thou clothed his neck with thunder? Canst thou make
him
afraid as a grasshopper? the glory of his nostrils is terrible. He
paweth in the valley, and rejoiceth in his strength, he goeth on to meet
the armed men. He mocketh at fear, and is not affrighted; neither
turneth he back from the sword. The quiver rattleth against him, the
glittering spear and the shield. He swalloweth the ground with
fierceness and rage: neither believeth he that it is the sound of the
trumpet. He saith among the trumpets, Ha, ha; and he smelleth the
battle
afar off, the thunder of the captains, and the shouting."

He alludes to a very beautiful wonder of his forming skill--"the
treasures of the snow." Few persons imagine the marvels of the fleecy
storm that whiten the earth in winter. What a variety of perfect
crystals! and how delicate their form and finish! The ice is made of
crystals, and often gives out aeolion music at the touch of winter. Even
the frost makes fine drawings on the window panes of leaves and flowers.

But the people of Palestine and the regions around it, know little of
our northern winters. The cold season is brief, and the occasional snow
storms light, and of short duration.

After God had finished his sublime appeal, Job bowed his head low
before
him, and declared that all he had known of him before, compared with
what he had learned since he was afflicted, was no more than hearing

about him; "for," he added, "now mine eye seeeth thee; wherefore I abhor
myself, and repent in dust and ashes."

Then the Lord rebuked Job's friends, because they had judged him
harshly, and "had multiplied words without knowledge," directing them to
offer a sacrifice for him.

The patriarch prospered again under Jehovah's smile, and became greater
in wealth, and family, and influence, than he was when Satan assailed
him. The deceiver and persecutor does not appear again in the annals of
the devout Arabian; disappointed and enraged, he turned his malice
against others more easily conquered and led captive by his wiles.

How awakening the thought that he still goes about "as a roaring lion,
seeking whom he may devour." But with loving trust in God, he can only
repeat his fruitless effort to destroy, preparing the way for richest
blessings.

Nathan Reproving David.

David's Charge to Solomon.

THE BIBLE AND THE HOLY LAND.

PATRIARCHS. KINGS. AND KINGDOMS.

THE FIRST KINGS.

Theocracy, we have seen, was the first form of government in the
world.

The word is from Theos, which means God; for He ruled by direct
command,
and would have continued to have been the only and perfect sovereign,
had not man been disloyal to him.

The patriarchal quay, which was that of the family, having at length
united households and extended authority, was still a Theocracy.

When God made his people a separate nation, each of the twelve tribes,
which sprang from the sons of Jacob, had its own ruler. If any important
matter concerning them all demanded public attention, they called an
assembly of their leaders.

When the bondage in Egypt was broken, Moses was the deliverer and
lawgiver of Israel, and Joshua the great general or military chieftain.

The high priest was the visible servant of God--his representative of
the Redeemer of his people.

Then came the judges, who were a kind of governors, having power to
declare war and make peace for the nation, but wearing no badges of
distinction. Jehovah revealed through them his will, and was still the
glorious king of Israel.

With the increase in numbers and general prosperity, there was a
decrease of the religious element and of harmony among the people.
They
also ceased to appreciate the simple and sublime principles of a
Theocracy, while all around them was the central power and the pomp

of
pagan monarchies; and they became tired of God's holy sovereignty,
having no visible display of authority. There were dissensions and civil
strife in Israel, in consequence of these departures from the Lord, and
strange melancholy blindness to their preeminence over other nations.

It was with them as it will be in the great American Republic, if
Puritan faith and works decline, until practical atheism prevails in our
"goodly land." The people will throw off wholesome restraints, become
divided North and South, and corrupt in morals, until a monarchy will
be
the natural resort of the people, as a protection against their own
selfish passions and conflicts.

Samuel, the wonderful child of Elkanah and Hannah, given to them,
like
Jephthah and Samson, as a special mark of divine favor, and who early
entered the temple-service under Eli, was the last of the judges,
excepting the authority which he delegated to his sons. He was a noble,
dutiful and devout boy, and a faithful priest and magistrate in Israel.
Eli, whose sons were dissipated, and slain by God's revealed purpose
on
account of their enemies, preceded him, so that Samuel saw the last of
the Theocracy, and inaugurated by the Lord's command a monarchy in
Palestine.

The Hebrews came to him begging for a king, and urging, as one reason
for the change, the unfitness of his sons to succeed him. They were
mercenary and open to bribery, and it is not strange that they were
disliked by the people. It is one of many instances of departure by
children from the counsels and prayers of the kindest parents, and
choosing the "wages of sin."

Samuel took the petition of the people to God for direction in answering
it. The Lord's message was the following:

"Hearken to the voice of the people in all that they say to thee: for
they have not rejected thee, but they have rejected me, that I should
not reign over them. According to all the works which they have done,
since the day that I brought them out of the land of Egypt, even to this
day, wherewith they have forsaken me, and served other gods, so do

they
also to thee. Now, therefore, hearken to their voice: nevertheless
testify solemnly to them, and show them the practice of the king that
shall reign over them."

He then enumerated the burdens of the state which they must bear. The
inventory of these royal exactions is so true to the experience of all
countries under kingly rule, you will read it with interest. It was the
first divine statement of the nature of a monarchy, and has needed no
important change in the progress of the ages. Jehovah told Samuel to
repeat the following description of the desired blessing, a king:

"He will take your sons and appoint them for himself, for his chariots,
and to be his horsemen; and some shall run before his chariots. And he
will appoint him captains over thousands, and captains over fifties; and
will set them to ear his ground, and to reap his harvest, and to make
his instruments of war and instruments of chariots. And he will take
your daughters to be confectioners, and to be cooks, and to be bakers.
And he will take your fields, and your vineyards, and your olive-yards,
even the best of them, and give them to his servants. And he will take
the tenth of your seed, and of your vineyards, and give them to his
officers, and to his servants; and he will take your men-servants, and
your maid-servants, and your goodliest young men, and your asses,
and
put them to his works. And he will take the tenth of your sheep: and ye
shall be his servants. And ye shall cry out in that day, beware of your
king which ye shall have chosen you; and the Lord will not hear you in
that day."

Saul and the Witch of Endor.

God had selected the first monarch of earth outside of heathenism. In the comparatively small tribe of Benjamin, was a man of honorable ancestry named Kish. His son, Saul, was a splendid young man, and would
have attracted admiring attention anywhere, and in any land under the sun, then or since his day. He was taller from his shoulders than all the rest of Israel's men, and possessed of the highest style of manly

beauty. Repeated mention is made of his noble figure and bearing. The providential circumstances which attended his promotion were re-markable.

He had wandered about for three days seeking the strayed asses of his father. Fatigued with the unsuccessful search, he was inclined to abandon it and return home, when, finding himself near Ramah, where Samuel lived, he resolved to consult one who was renowned in all Israel as a man from whom nothing was hid. Instructed in the divine designs regarding Saul, the prophet received him with honor. He assured him that
the asses which he had sought were already found, and invited him to stay with him until the next morning. Saul was in fact the man on whom
the divine appointment to be the first king of Israel had fallen. A hint of this high destiny produced from the astonished stranger a modest declaration of his insufficiency. But the prophet gave him the place of honor before all the persons whom--foreknowing the time of his arrival--
he had invited to his table. As is still usual in summer, Saul slept on the flat roof of the house; and was called early in the morning by Samuel, who walked forth some way with him on his return home. When they
had got beyond the town they stopped, and Samuel then anointed Saul as
the person whom God had chosen to be "captain over his inheritance;" and
gave him the first kiss of civil homage. In token of the reality of these things, and to assure the mind of the bewildered young man, the prophet foretold the incidents of his homeward journey, and, in part-ing,
desired his attendance on the seventh day following at Gilgal.

On the day and at the place appointed, Samuel assembled a general convocation of the tribes for the election of a king. As usual, under the Theocracy, the choice of God was manifested by the sacred lot. The tribe of Benjamin was chosen; and of the families of Benjamin, that of Matri was taken; and, finally, the lot fell upon the person of Saul, the son of Kish. Anticipating this result, he had modestly concealed himself to avoid an honor which he so little desired. But he was found and

brought before the people, who beheld with enthusiasm his finely developed form and preeminence in appearance, and hailed him as their
king.

Many prominent persons of the great tribes were jealous and indignant, because the smallest tribe, and a young man whose chief claim to the honor was his fine figure, had been chosen. They refused to join the masses in their homage, and Saul displayed his shrewdness in "holding his peace."

And the wisdom of God was apparent in the result; for he gradually united the discordant elements around him, and became established in power. Soon after came the trial of his ability as a general.

The Ammonites, a mighty and warlike people under king Nahash, besieged
the important town of Jabesh-Gilead. The beleaguered place was at length
compelled to ask terms of capitulation. The proud and cruel reply was, that every man should have his right eye put out.

The Jabesh-Gileadites agreed to the hard conditions, unless help reached
them within seven days. Messengers hastened to Saul, in Gibeah, and found him returning from his herds in the field. The story of the invasion and peril roused all the energies and martial spirit of a king worthy of his crown.  It was the Lord's inspiration for his high office, and immediate command of the army.

The inhabitants were timid; and to awaken their courage he slew oxen, had them quartered, and sent the pieces over the kingdom, assuring those
who were able to fight, that unless they hastened to the rescue all their cattle should have a similar slaughter. The volunteers came pouring in, and Saul marched to Jabesh-Gilead. A battle followed, and the Ammonites were routed with terrible slaughter. It was a grand victory, and won for Saul the glory of military genius. This settled the question of his right to reign, and his sceptre was held over an undivided people.

Retaining three thousand men, he followed up the conquest by an attack
upon the Philistines, who had conquered on the south, and deprived
Israel of weapons of war, and implements of husbandry. Only Saul and
Jonathan had either sword or spear. The latter, a gifted and noble young
man, distinguished himself, under God's special benediction, in a
successful assault upon a garrison of the Philistines. The enemy rallied
in full strength, and Saul prepared to meet them with additional forces.

Samuel had appointed sacrifices to be made before the campaign was
opened, and because he did not appear in Gilgal when Saul expected
him,
the king turned priest, and presented the offerings. This rashness
revealed his undevout character and haughty self-will, which proved
his
ruin.

Saul Rejected.

Meanwhile the most of his troops had scattered, through fear of the
powerful foe. But Jonathan determined to make a bold onset, and, with

his armor-bearer, climbed a high cliff, and fell upon the Philistines.
They supposed the Hebrews were rushing from ambush upon them, and began
to fly. Saul entered the field and aided in the overthrow of the
defeated warriors, slaying and treading each other down in the wild
confusion of the retreat.

During the last years of Saul's reign, conscious that God had forsaken
him, in one of his campaigns against the Philistines he sought the
counsel of a witch. When he beheld the vast force which the Philistine
states had, by a mighty effort, brought into the field, dire misgivings
as to the result arose in his mind; and now, at last, in this extremity,
he sought counsel of God. But the Lord answered him not by any of the
usual means--by dreams, by Urim, or by prophets. Finding himself thus
forsaken, he had recourse to a witch at Endor, not far from Gilboa, to
whom he repaired by night in disguise, and conjured her to evoke the
spirit of Samuel, that he might ask counsel of him in this fearful
emergency. Accordingly, an aged and mantled figure arose, which Saul
took to be the ghost of Samuel, though whether it were really so or not
has been much questioned. The king bowed himself reverently, and told
the reason for which he had called him from the dead. The figure, in
reply, told him that God had taken the crown from his house, and given
it to a worthier man; that, on the next day, the Philistines would
triumph over Israel; and that he and his sons should be slain in the
battle. The king swooned at these heavy tidings, but soon recovered,
and, having taken some refreshment, returned the same night to the
camp.

The engraver's art has produced a picture of this strange scene, one
which cannot be clearly and satisfactorily explained.

Saul received orders, through Samuel, to execute the Lord's "fierce
wrath" upon the Amelekites, who had formerly been doomed to utter
extermination, for opposing the Israelites when they came out of Egypt.
The result of the war put it fully in the king's power to fulfil his
commission; but he retained the best of the cattle as booty, and brought
back the Amalekite king Agag as a prisoner. Here Saul again ventured to
use his own discretion where his commission left him none. For this the
divine decree, excluding his descendants from the throne, was again

and
irrevocably pronounced by Samuel, who met him at Gilgal on his return.
The stern prophet then directed the Amalekite king to be brought forth
and slain by the sword, after which he departed to his own home, and
went no more to see Saul to the day of his death, though he ceased not
to bemoan his misconduct, and the forfeiture it had incurred.

The next engraving is a very good view of this crisis in Saul's
destiny--his rejection by God and his prophet. When Samuel turned to
leave the king, the terrified ruler seized his mantle, and in the
struggle it was torn. The prophet improved the incident by telling him
that thus should his kingdom be rent from him, and given to a neighbor.

We cannot follow Saul through all the achievements and crimes of his
eventful reign; the abandonment of him by the grieved and indignant
Samuel; his deceptive prosperity; and his conscious desertion by God,
until his fits of depression bordered on madness. He had genius and
heroism, but a bad heart, and the hour of his overthrow drew near.

The venerable and gifted prophet who anointed the king was commanded by
Jehovah to consecrate the successor to the throne. He was directed to go
to Bethlehem, and there anoint one of the sons of Jesse. He knew that
should Saul be informed of the errand, his days were numbered. The
doom
of a traitor would follow the solemn act.

To protect his servant the Lord told Samuel to offer a sacrifice, and
tell the king he was going to Bethlehem for the purpose.

When Samuel reached Bethlehem, he laid the offerings upon the altar,
and
invited a worthy citizen and his family to the sacrifice. The good man's
name was Jesse, and he had eight sons. Eliab, the eldest, like Saul, was
fine-looking--tall, athletic, and commanding in his personal appearance.
Samuel thought he must be the future king of Israel; but God revealed
to
him his mistake. Six brothers followed him in their presentation to the
prophet, and the Lord gave the same intimation of his will he had

respecting Eliab.

The man of God was perplexed. What could he do, if these were the only
sons of Jesse, as it seemed, for no more came? It occurred to him,
however, that possibly there might be another boy, and he inquired of
Jesse if it were not so.

The excellent father had sent the youngest son, about fifteen years old,
to keep the sheep, and it did not even enter his mind that this mere
child could have any thing to do with the affairs of the kingdom. He
stated the facts to Samuel, who immediately desired to see the lad. He
was sent for, and soon stood before the prophet. The patriarchal servant
of the Infinite One looked upon the noble boy, with his "ruddy and
beautiful countenance," and saw in him the next monarch of Israel.

Christ Blessing Little Children.

David stood among his brethren, a modest, bewildered shepherd boy,
uninjured by unholy gratification of passion and appetite--a
pure-minded, manly, and devout youth.

God told Samuel to anoint him, and he poured the consecrating oil
upon
the fair brow of the astonished David. Then the Spirit of the Lord came

upon him, and departed from Saul altogether. The juvenile shepherd and
hero, who had slain a lion and a bear, in defence of his sheep, returned to his flocks, a king in destiny.

Remorse, the predictions of Samuel against him, and baleful passions, made Saul so wretchedly melancholy, that some of his attendants suggested to the monarch that he should try the soothing effect of music. The proposition was favorably received, and upon the recommendation of another friend, David, the son of Jesse, of whom Saul
knew nothing before, was sent for to play upon the harp. The young minstrel won the respect and affection of the royal household, and his harpings were the principal solace of the infatuated and gloomy king, who at length made David his armor-bearer.

You know the warriors of ancient time wore armor made of metal to protect the body from the spear and sword, the common weapons of the
battle-field; and men were appointed by monarchs to have the care of it.

Since their last great discomfiture, the Philistines had recruited their strength, and in the thirtieth year of Saul's reign, and the twentieth of David's life, they again took the field against the Israelites. It curiously illustrates the nature of warfare in those times, to find that the presence, in the army of the Philistines, of one enormous giant, about nine or ten feet high, filled them with confidence, and struck the Israelites with dread. Attended by his armor-bearer, and clad in complete mail, with weapons to match his huge bulk, the giant, whose name was Goliah, presented himself daily between the two armies, and, with insulting language, defied the Israelites to produce a champion who, by single combat, might decide the quarrel between the nations. This was repeated many days; but no Israelite was found bold enough to
accept the challenge. At length David, who had come to the battle-field with food for his brethren, no longer able to endure the taunts and blasphemies of Goliah, offered himself for the combat. The king, contrasting the size and known prowess of the giant with the youth and inexperience of Jesse's son, dissuaded him from the enterprise. But as David expressed his strong confidence that the God of Israel, who had delivered him from the lion and the bear, when he tended his father's

flock, would also deliver him from the proud Philistine, Saul at length
allowed him to go forth against Goliah. Refusing all armor of proof, and
weapons of common warfare, David advanced to the combat, armed
only with
his shepherd's sling, and a few smooth pebbles picked up from the
brook
which flowed through the valley. The astonished giant felt insulted at
such an opponent, and poured forth such horrid threats as might have
appalled anyone less strong in faith than the son of Jesse. But as he
strode forward to meet David, the latter slung one of his smooth stones
with so sure an aim and so strong an arm, that it smote his opponent in
the middle of the forehead, and brought him to the ground.

The praises of the people lavished on David excited Saul's jealousy, and
he sought in various ways to kill David, who seemed to have a charmed
life; for God was with him, and no blow aimed at his life was
successful.

The king's son, Jonathan, loved David devotedly, and more than once
saved him from the wrath of Saul.

After hunting the son of Jesse, consulting witches in his desperation,
and fighting the Philistines in bloody conflicts, near Mount Gilboa,
defeated and wounded, he committed suicide by falling on his sword.
Thus
ended the career of the first king of the Hebrew nation.

David, under divine guidance, went to Hebron, and was there publicly
anointed king by the tribe of Judah. But Abner, a splendid general, and
a great friend of Saul, induced the rest of the tribes to acknowledge
Ishbosheth, the only son of Saul then living, as their sovereign. Soon,
however, a quarrel with his protege, led him to join David, who was at
length proclaimed king by all the people.

After years of prosperity in war and peace, he had a sanguinary battle
with the Ammonites. This occurred in the eighteenth year of his reign.
The conduct of this war David intrusted to Joab, and remained himself
at
Jerusalem. There, while sauntering upon the roof of his palace, after
the noonday sleep, which is usual in the East, he perceived a woman
whose great beauty attracted his regard. She proved to be Bathsheba,

the
wife of Uriah, an officer of Canaanitish origin, then absent with the
army besieging Rabbah, the capital of Ammon. David was so fascinated
with her that he determined to add her to his royal household. He sent
for Uriah to Jerusalem. Having heard from him the particulars of the
war, which he pretended to require, the king dismissed him to his own
home. But Uriah, feeling that it ill became a soldier to seek his bed
while his companions lay on the hard ground, under the canopy of
heaven,
exposed to the attacks of the enemy, remained all night in the hall of
the palace with the guards, and returned to the war without having
seen
Bathsheba. David made him the bearer of an order to Joab to expose
him
to certain death, in some perilous enterprize against the enemy. He was
obeyed by that unscrupulous general; and when David heard that
Uriah was
dead, he sent for Bathsheba, and made her his wife. He had already
several wives, as was customary in those times; and among them was
Michal, whom he had long ago reclaimed from the man to whom she
had been
given by the unprincipled Saul.

The Woman of Canaan.

David, whose undisputed authority, and admiration of the beautiful Bathsheba, deceived him, blinding his moral vision, thought all was safe. Death and royalty seemed to cover forever his sin.

But never was a man more mistaken. God sent Nathan, a fearless, faithful
prophet, to rebuke him. So the seer went to him, inquiring what should be done with a man who had robbed a poor neighbor of his only and pet
lamb. The king, who was really loyal to God, and just in his aims, indignantly said that the robber should die, and the lamb be restored. Then Nathan fixed his eye on the king, and, pointing to him, exclaimed courageously, "Thou art the man!"

David bowed his head and wept under the pointed reproof, and began to
cry, "Deliver me from blood-guiltiness, oh, God, thou God of my salvation."

What a fine example of faithful preaching, and of an honest hearer! This illustration of true penitence, which is given in the picture at the beginning of this history of the kings, suggests a good story of modern date. Jacob, an intelligent negro, was bribed and intoxicated to make him commit murder. He was convicted of the crime, and sent to the State
prison for life. He could not read, but a bible was in his cell, and he learned so rapidly that soon he could pick out the words and get the meaning. He would run his finger over each letter of the fifty-first Psalm, especially the fourteenth verse, until he enamelled it with his touch. The bible is still kept by an excellent man, as a relic of prison-life. For Jacob was pardoned, went to the lovely town of C-, N.Y.,  and became an eminent Christian. His monument is one of the highest in the cemetery.

The Scriptures describe David as "a man after God's own heart." By this we are not to understand that David always acted rightly, or that God approved of all he did. Its meaning is, that, in his public capacity, as king of Israel, he acted in accordance with the true theory of the theocratical government; was always alive to his dependence on the Supreme King; took his own true place in the system, and aspired to no other; and conducted all his undertakings with reference to the Supreme
Will. He constantly calls himself "the servant (or vassal) of Jehovah," and that, and no other, was the true place for the human king of Israel to fill. In thus limiting the description of David as "a man after God's own heart," it is not necessary for us to vindicate all his acts, or to uphold him as an immaculate character. But the same ardent tempera-
ment
which sometimes betrayed his judgment in his public acts, led him into great errors and crimes. It also made him the first to discover his lapse, and the last to forgive himself.

Domestic afflictions humbled David, and persecution by enemies embittered his life. The kingly crown had its thorns. An only child died in infancy. Afterwards, his handsome and popular son, Absalom, was ambitious to get the throne of his father, and became the leader of a great revolt, in whose conflicts he was slain.

Solomon, another son, was the heir chosen by the Lord, to the crown of

David. And when the monarch of Israel drew near the close of his stormy,
yet splendid reign, he called the intellectual, comely, and dutiful boy
to his bedside, to give him his last words of counsel and blessing.

This scene is depicted in the colored engraving. Among the paternal
exhortations to the young prince was the following impressive address:
"And thou, Solomon, my son, know thou the God of thy fathers, and serve
him with a perfect heart, and with a willing mind; for the Lord
searcheth all hearts, and understandeth all the imaginations of the
thoughts. If thou seek him, he will be found of thee but if thou forsake
him, he will cast thee off forever."

Solomon, the second king of Israel, desired and sought, before riches
and honors, wisdom from God, to govern well the people, and it was
freely given.

Under his father's sceptre, Palestine was great in martial achievements,
national wealth, and the fine arts; for the king was a poet and a
musician. Solomon was a man of peace, and during his reign the king-dom
reached its highest glory in oriental splendor and luxury. The temple he
built was a monument of munificence, skill, and royal zeal for God's
honor.

What a wonderful display of wisdom was that decision in the case of the
two women, one of whom, in her sleep, lying upon her babe, had smothered
it, and claimed the living child of the other, who lodged with her. He
knew when he sent for the executioner, and told him to cut in two parts
the live babe, giving to each a half, that the mother would be seen in
the effect of the command to slay. And so it was. The faithless woman
said let it be so; the loving, yearning mother exclaimed no, rather let
the other have the child. Solomon wisely decided the matter, directing
the attendants to give the unconscious object of controversy to her to
whom it belonged.

But this rich and popular monarch was led into sin by his unbounded
prosperity, and indulging in forbidden pleasures. Afterwards he bitter-

ly
mourned over his folly and shameful weakness, in departing from the
living God. This varied and, much of it, wasted life, led the king, in
his sober years of declining age, to write the Book of Proverbs and
Ecclesiastes, so full of the profoundest knowledge of mankind and
wisest
counsel. It is said that the Scotch are preeminently discerning and
intelligent, because they are so familiar with the Scriptures,
especially the proverbs of Solomon.

There were no more such monarchs in Israel, after David and Solomon,
and
the kingdom became divided and weakened, until the Jews were conquered
and enslaved by their enemies. The expensive magnificence and luxury
of
Solomon's reign, and his departures from God into idolatrous worship,
awakened the divine indignation.

A prophet was commissioned to tell the wise, yet foolish monarch that
the kingdom should be rent in twain, and the grandeur of his empire
depart before the revolt of the ten tribes from Judah, which had
absorbed the small tribe of Benjamin. Solomon was about sixty years
old
when he died. He had ruled forty years, and was buried nine hundred
and
seventy-five years before the advent of Christ. Rehoboam, the son of
Solomon, was made king over Judah, and Jereboam, an Ephraimite,
became
sovereign of the ten tribes, who were called Israel.

How interesting and instructive the history of the Hebrews, at this
period!

They got tired of the sovereignty of God, visible only in written rules
of conduct, family government, and the prophet-judges, and desired to
imitate their pagan neighbors in the pomp and power of royalty. Under
their second monarch they quarrelled among themselves, engaged in
civil
strife, and became divided, rival kingdoms. During the five hundred
years which followed, the successive kings of the two realms had, the

most of them, brief sovereignty. Some of them were excellent kings, but the greater part were wicked and oppressive.

Pre-eminent in crime was Ahab, whose wife, Jezebel, was a fit companion.

Their names live in the world's history with a bad preeminence, like those of Herod, Nero, and similar rulers of ancient and modern times.

The corpse of a ruler, or of the humblest subject, was ordinarily wound in grave-clothes, and laid in a sepulchre. This, in the early ages, was a room hewn out of a rock, a cave, or a grave which had no mound, nor any other mark, excepting monumental stones, with no inscriptions.

The Arabian patriarch, Job, talked of kings and counsellors, who built for themselves "desolate places," which probably has reference to sepulchral monuments, cut out of the rock.

The expression "a sepulchre on high," is an allusion to the custom anciently of placing the dead in tombs made in cliffs, sometimes hundreds of feet in height--a lofty, inaccessible resting-place for the body of a distinguished person.

Some nations of the heathen world have always burned their dead. In Japan, recently, an American traveller witnessed this singular disposal of the lifeless remains. A priest was placed in a sitting posture in his coffin, and a fire built behind it, consuming to ashes the body. These relics were carefully gathered up, and put in a safe and sacred place for all coming time.

It is a remarkable thing that the Bible does not record any solemn parade or imposing ceremonies over the burial of the Hebrew kings.

Of David it is written, he "slept with his fathers, and was buried in the city of David." The same simple and impressive mention is made of Solomon's death. Monarchs were only men--sinners to be saved by grace,
if rescued at all from the power and ruin of sin. It is hoped and believed by Christian people that Solomon, in his declining years, reviewed prayerfully and penitently his career, and found peace with a pardoning God.

The sepulchre of royalty in Jerusalem, is well worthy of a visit by travellers in the Holy Land. Some of the stone coffins lean against the solid walls, others lie in massive richness of sculpture on the floor.

The Jews called their burial places the house of the living, because of the expected resurrection--a beautiful sentiment, which rebukes the dismal thoughts and mourning of many Christian persons over the newly
made graves of their departed friends.

The beautiful tomb in the "valley of Jehosaphat," is one of comparatively modern construction, but it shows the admiration felt by the Hebrews for Absalom, with all his waywardness.

Joseph Elevated to Power by Pharaoh.

The Israelites Carried into Captivity.

THE BIBLE AND THE HOLY LAND.

PATRIARCHS, KINGS AND KINGDOMS.

PALESTINE UNDER PAGAN KINGS.

The picture which introduces these pages was drawn from a scene under
the sceptre of the first monarch mentioned in the Bible.

A comparatively unimportant prince, the "King of Sodom," whose small and
wicked realm Jehovah destroyed by fire and brimstone, is mentioned.

But the empire of the Pharaohs of Egypt, was large, rich, and
magnificent. And it is a singular thing, that of this nation, and all
others of antiquity, excepting what the Scriptures contain, the early
history is little known. A great German historian, Dr. Von Rotteck,
truly writes: "The principal trait that distinguishes the first period
of the ancient world is its obscurity."

The general belief is, that the founders of Egypt went from Ethiopia,
and the Ethiopians from East India or South Arabia.

"Where did the Indiamen have their origin?" you may ask; but no man can
certainly answer. That all races sprang from Adam we have no doubt, but
the lines of descent and emigration the wisest student of the past
cannot follow.

The living oracles, in brief statements, give us nearly all the reliable
accounts we have of the early history of the "Land of the Nile," as
Egypt was called. In them we learn that while the "chosen people of
God," the only nation whose annals of growth in the number of its
population and its civilization, has been handed down to us, was no more
than a tribe of wandering shepherds under Abraham, Egypt was the home of
art, and a garden of agricultural products.

And yet the very nomades, who roamed over the uncultivated plains, like
the Aborigines of this new world, have preserved the best records of the
early condition of that ancient and wonderful empire, whose origin is
lost in the distance and darkness of Pagan antiquities.

It seems, from the tenth chapter of Genesis, that Egypt was settled by
the descendants of Noah, through Ham, his second son.

The next reference made to this remarkable country is in the twelfth
chapter, where we are told of Abraham's visit there. Again, in the
twenty-first chapter, is recorded the marriage of Ishmael to an Egyptian
woman. In chapter twenty-ninth is related the story of Joseph's
captivity and career in the capital of the Pagan monarchy. He was the
twelfth son of Jacob, and one of Rachel's two boys--lovely in his
youthful character, and the idol of his father. During a period of
repose in sleep he had a singular dream. The first was, that while the
brothers were all in the harvest-field at work his sheaf suddenly rose
upright, and the sheaves of the eleven brethren stood up and bowed to
his own. The intimation that he was to rule over them made them an-gry,
and they hated him.

Soon after Joseph's sleep he was disturbed by another dream. The sun,
moon, and eleven stars, rendered homage to him. The interpretation of
this was the same as that of the other, with the addition of his father
and mother, who also bowed before him.

It may seem strange that Joseph should relate any thing so complimen-tary
to himself. But he evidently did it in no boasting mood. He simply
narrated the extraordinary dreams, without the least idea of what was
before him.

But God saw what he did hot know, that their jealousy and enmity would
be overruled for the temporal salvation of the family and nation.

The venerable, thoughtful father, silently pondered over the singular
experience of Joseph.

The elder sons were shepherds, and fed their flocks in Shechem. How beautiful the ingenious, dutiful character of Joseph now appears! His father called him to go and find his brethren, to see how they were getting along. "Here am I," was his response. That is to say: "Although my brethren hate me, I am ready to serve you, and do any thing for them." He went to Shechem, but they had left; and the boy wandered about
in the field looking for them. A citizen happened to see him, and was evidently interested in the beautiful stranger, bewildered and alone, and asked what he wanted. Joseph told him the truth of the case, when the man said that his brothers had taken their flocks to Dotham, a few miles distant.

He started for that place, and while a "great way off," they saw and knew him. The conspiracy was instantly formed to dispose of the "dreamer."

The first proposition was to kill him, but Reuben would not agree to the cruel suggestion. His plan was to cast the lad into a deep pit, till he could manage to get him back to his father. This less bloody way of disposing of Joseph was accepted, and when he came near they took off the "coat of many colors" the doting father had given him, and putting him in a pit without water which happened to be at hand, dipping it in blood to make his father think a beast killed him, they took it home. Scarcely was the interesting boy weeping in his prison before a caravan of Ishmaelites, and then of Midianites, came in sight.

Moses Found in the Bulrushes.

A new idea now flashed upon their minds. They could avoid the un-
pleasant
consciousness of probable murder, and make something out of his sale
as
a slave to the wandering traders. A bargain was soon made, and young
Joseph, casting backward a farewell look of sad reproach, was carried
away, and sold by the Midianites to the Ishmaelites, of whom Potiphar,
the captain of Pharaoh's guard, bought him for a servant. God blessed
the youth, and he was soon made overseer of the officer's household.
But
Potiphar's wife was a vile woman, and because Joseph was nobly true
to
God and virtue, made a false report of him, and had him put in prison.

Egypt's monarch had wonderful dreams about a famine his astrologers
could not explain; and a released prisoner, who had forgotten Joseph's
kindness in explaining a dream of deliverance, advised the king to send
for the Hebrew. The young man was taken to the palace, and gave a
true

interpretation of the dreams. Pharaoh was delighted; and from his dungeon Joseph went to the secret place of authority second to the king. Pharaoh said: "Only in the throne will I be greater than thou." He then put a ring on his finger, a gold chain on his neck, and arrayed him in fine apparel. The beautiful illustration sets this sudden and splendid promotion before us--the honor God put upon his youthful servant.

Soon the predicted famine came, for which the gifted and prudent Joseph
had made complete provision by storing up the abundant harvests.
Among
the sufferers from failing crops and pasturage, was the large family of Jacob--his sons and their households.

In their extremity they turned to Egypt. Joseph's influence was such that the patriarch's delegation found favor with the king. The prime-minister of Egypt knew his brethren, but they had forgotten him. So he managed to find out all about his father's house, and made his brothers bring dear Benjamin, when he wept aloud, and made himself known
to them all. Pharaoh sent for the whole race, and soon the Hebrew caravan reached the fruitful land of Goshen, which was exactly suited
to
the life of shepherds. Here the strangers grew in numbers and wealth, until Joseph died, and the friendly monarch also. His successor cared neither for Joseph nor his countrymen. He was a tyrant, and enslaved the
dwellers in Goshen. Centuries of captivity wore away, and God deter-
mined
to deliver his people, and send them back again to Palestine.

The scene displayed in this picture you will recognize at a glance. Moses, the Hebrew babe, afloat on the Nile, in a small boat made of bulrushes by his mother, because Pharaoh was slaying the children of her
nation, to get rid of them.

Neither the haughty and cruel monarch, nor the mother, nor the little voyager, thought of Moses as the future deliverer of his countrymen from
bondage--the great leader and lawgiver of Israel.

We have already had glimpses of the Hebrews in the wilderness, their progress and rulers in Palestine, after the moving multitude reached the "promised land."

The ages of changing sovereigns, and fortunes of crimes and discipline brought them at last to another mournful captivity.

About six hundred years before Christ, while that wicked Manassah was
king in Palestine, the monarch of Assyria--a grand and powerful empire--invaded it, and took Jerusalem. Manassah was carried in chains to Babylon, the splendid Assyrian capital. His son, Amon, became the sovereign under the Assyrian conqueror, but was soon assassinated, and
Josiah took the throne.

During his reign, the King of Egypt marched into Palestine and con-quered
it, killing Josiah, the king.

A few years later, Nebuchadnezzar, the Babylonian monarch, besieged and
took Jerusalem, the "City of David."

The massive walls of the cities of old was their chief protection. Those of Babylon, according to the old Roman historians, were marvelously great. Think of them rising three hundred and fifty feet, eighty-seven feet in thickness, and extending sixty miles around the city! One writer says, that two four-horse chariots could pass each other on the top. They were built of brick, cemented together with bitumen.

They had twenty gates made of solid brass, and were surmounted with two
hundred and fifty towers.

The city had six hundred and seventy-six squares, each over two miles in
circumference. The river Euphrates flowed through the entire extent, from north to south.

The hanging gardens, suspended from the walls, were gorgeous, and the
public buildings rich and elegant.

Such was the home of the Hebrew exiles for seventy years or more.

Quintus Curtius, a Roman, has described the entrance of the great and
victorious Alexander into Babylon, at a later period, who soon after
died there of dissipation, while yet a young man. The pleasant sketch
gives a vivid impression of the glory and pomp of this ancient capital
of Babylon:

Christ Declaring Who is Greatest.

"A great part of the inhabitants of Babylon stood on the walls, eager to
catch a sight of their new monarch; many went forth to meet him.
Among
these Bagophanes, keeper of the citadel and of the royal treasure,
strewed the entire way before the king with flowers and crowns; silver

altars were also placed on both sides of the road, which were loaded not merely with frankincense, but all kinds of odoriferous herbs. He brought
with him for Alexander gifts of various kinds, flocks of sheep and horses; lions, also, and panthers were carried before him in their dens. The magi came next, singing in their usual manner their ancient hymns. After them came the Chaldeans with their musical instruments, who are not only the prophets of the Babylonians, but their artists. The first are wont to sing the praises of the kings; the Chaldeans teach the motion of the stars, and the changes of the seasons. Then followed, last of all, the Babylonian knights, whose equipments, as well as that of their horses, showed the passion of the people for luxury. The king, Alexander, attended by armed men, having ordered the crowd of the townspeople to proceed in the rear of his infantry, entered the city in a chariot and repaired to the palace. The next day he carefully surveyed the household treasures of Darius, and all his money. For the rest, the beauty of the city and its age turned the eyes not only of the king, but of everyone in itself, and that with good reason."

The kings and conquerors of old had no canals for boats, no railways, and not many good roads. Consequently, their invasions and various public enterprises were carried forward in a slow and toilsome manner. Heavy wagons and chariots, the latter sometimes armed with scythes or long blades for battle, were the best vehicles in use.

There were no monitors, nor fire-arms. Large swords, daggers, slings, the catapulta and battering-ram, were the principal weapons.

The last named instrument was a massive machine with a movable beam,
crowned with a very hard end, often shaped like a ram's head, which could be thrown against a wall with tremendous force, beating it down.

The catapulta, which was placed upon city walls, was a great cross-bow for hurling arrows upon an enemy. In it was combined the bow and arrow,
and the sling. The mammoth arrow was put in the groove, the twisted ropes were connected with levers, and the powerful recoil would send the
strong and sharp arrow a great distance.

Some of the machines were large enough to discharge beams loaded with
iron; and one kind, called the balista, would send great stones,
crushing through the houses on which they fell.

Among the spoil, taken by Nebuchadnezzar to Babylon, were the costly
vessels of the temple; and he graced his train with members of the royal
family and the principal nobles.

He placed Zedekiah on the throne of his Hebrew province, who soon after
rebelled against him.

In consequence of this revolt, the Babylonian king invaded Judea with a
great army, and, after taking most of the principal towns, sat down
before Jerusalem. Early in the next year the Egyptians marched an army
to the relief of their ally, but being intimidated by the alacrity with
which the Babylonians raised the siege and advanced to give them battle,
they returned home without risking an engagement. The return of the
Chaldeans to the siege, destroyed all the hopes which the approach of
the Egyptian succors had excited. The siege was now prosecuted with
redoubled vigor; and at length Jerusalem was taken by storm at mid-
night,
in the eleventh year of Zedekiah, and in the eighteenth month from the
commencement of the siege. Dreadful was the carnage. The people, young
and old, were slaughtered wherever they appeared; and even the temple
was no refuge for them; the sacred courts streamed with blood. Zedekiah
himself, with his family and some friends, contrived to escape from the
city; but he was overtaken and captured in the plains of Jericho. He was
sent in chains to Nebuchadnezzar, who had left the conclusion of the
war
to his generals, and was then at Riblah in Syria. After sternly
reproving him for his ungrateful conduct, the conqueror ordered all the
sons of Zedekiah to be slain before his eyes, and then his own eyes to
be put out, thus making the slaughter of his children the last sight on
which his tortured memory could dwell. He was afterward sent in fetters

of brass to Babylon, where he remained until his death.

Nebuchadnezzar evidently felt that his purposes had not been fully
executed by the army, or else he was urged by the Edomites and others
to
exceed his first intentions. He therefore sent Nebuzaradan, the captain
of the guard, with a sufficient force to complete the desolation of
Judah and Jerusalem. He burned the city and the temple to the ground;
he
collected and sent to Babylon all the gold and silver which former
spoilers had left; and he transported all the people who had been left
behind in Jehoiachin's captivity, save only the poor of the land, who
were left to be vine-dressers and husbandmen. Four years after,
Nebuzaradan again entered Judea, and gleaned a few more of the miserable
inhabitants, whom he sent off to Babylon.

The Handwriting on the Wall.

Thus was the land left desolate; and thus ended the kingdom of Judah

and
the reign of David's house, after it had endured four hundred and four
years under twenty kings. It is remarkable that the King of Babylon
made
no attempt to colonize the country he had depopulated, as was done by
the Assyrians in Israel; and thus, in the providence of God, the land
was left vacant, to be re-occupied by the Jews after seventy years of
captivity and punishment.

The grand and melancholy march into captivity is seen in the
illustration of the artist.

What a vast and sad procession! The conquerors ride proudly on the
high
ground with the captive host in full view. The tower of Babel and the
walls of their magnificent city are visible in the distance.

The exiles found in Babylon many of their countrymen, who had been
carried there in previous conquests, and were useful, respectable
citizens. Among these, there was a young man of splendid abilities and
noble heart, named Daniel.

He was one of the youthful sons of high family, who were carried away
as
hostages for the fidelity of King Jehoiachin. He and some others were
put under the chief eunuch, to be properly trained in the language and
learning of the Chaldeans, to fit them for employments at the court.
This training lasted three years, when they were examined in the
presence of the king; and Daniel and three of his friends were found to
have made far greater progress than any of those who had been educat-
ed
with them. They were therefore enrolled among the magians or learned
men.

A few years after, Nebuchadnezzar was greatly troubled with a dream,
which made a profound impression upon his mind; but the particulars
of
which quite passed from his memory when he awoke. Great importance was
attached to dreams in those days, and men skilled in the sciences were
supposed to be able to discover their meaning. Therefore, the king sent

for his court magians, and required them not only to interpret the dream, but to discover the dream itself, which he had forgotten. This they declared to be impossible; on which the exasperated tyrant ordered
all the magians to be massacred. Daniel and his friends, although not present, were included in such a sentence. On learning this, he begged a respite for the whole body, undertaking to find, through his God, the solution of the difficulty. The respite was granted; and at the earnest prayer of Daniel, God made the secret known to him. A colossal image which the king saw, with a head of gold, arms and breast of silver, belly and thighs of brass, legs of iron, and toes partly iron and partly clay, was struck down by a stone, which itself grew and filled the whole earth. This, in the interpretation of Daniel, figured forth "the things to come;" describing by characteristic symbols the succession of empires to the end of time; and it is wonderful to observe how precisely the greater part of what was then future has since been accomplished. The king was not only satisfied but astonished; he was almost ready to pay divine honors to Daniel; and raised him at once to the eminent station of Archimagus, or chief of the magians, and governor of the metropolitan
province of Babylon. His three friends, also, were at his request, promoted to places of trust and honor.

Not long after, Nebuchadnezzar set up a colossal image in the plains of Dura, and commanded that, when music sounded, everyone should worship
it, on pain of death. He soon learned that this command was utterly neglected by Daniel's three friends, Shadrach, Meshach, and Abednego; and his rage grew so high, at the example of disobedience given by persons in their high station that he ordered them to be at once cast into "the burning furnace." The heat of the furnace was so great as to destroy the men who cast them in; but they themselves remained unhurt,
and not even a hair of their heads was singed. They came forth when the
king called them; and he was so much astonished and convinced by this prodigy, that he publicly acknowledged the greatness of the God whom they served.

There appear to have been good and generous qualities in the character of Nebuchadnezzar; but the pride with which he contemplated the

grandeur
of his empire, and the magnificence of his undertakings, was most
inordinate, and he required to be taught that "the Most High ruleth over
all the kingdoms of the earth, and giveth them to whomsoever he will."
He was warned of this in a dream, which was interpreted to him by
Daniel; but, neglecting the warning, "his heart was changed from man's,
and a beast's heart was given to him." He was afflicted with a madness
which made him think himself a beast, and, acting as such, he remained
constantly abroad in the fields, living upon wild herbs. In this debased
and forlorn condition the mighty conqueror remained seven years,
when he
was restored to his reason and his throne, and one of his first acts was
to issue a proclamation, humbly acknowledging the signs and wonders
which the Most High God had wrought toward him, and declaring his
conviction, that "those who walk in pride he is able to abase." He died
soon after.

The next illustration is drawn from the interpretation of the dream in
the royal palace. Conscious of Jehovah's favor and guidance, how
courageously and grandly he stands before the monarch, and declares
the
whole counsel of God!

He thus became a prophet of the Most High, whose wonderful career
afterwards, we shall again follow, when we come to the narratives of
the
seers.

The Vision of the Dragon Chained.

The spirit alienation from God, and of depraved desires, which ruled
the
ancient pagan realms is set before us under various titles. Among them
is that of the dragon, in the engraving; which the "king of kings" shall
yet bind forever and imprison.

The fate of the proud kingdoms which ruled Palestine, teaches the
world
how little importance God attaches to human glory in his punishment
of
the wicked.

Egypt has scarcely more than its location and name left. Its pyramids,
one of which it is estimated employed three hundred thousand men
twenty
years in building, stand in the desert places, solitary and pillaged
sepulchres.

The temple of Karnak, on the east bank of the Nile, whose massive

stone
roof was supported by one hundred and thirty-four majestic columns,
forty-three feet high, and ranged in sixteen rows; the whole structure
twelve hundred feet in length, and covered with figures of gods and
heroes; is one of the grandest works of time.

Should you visit the gorges of the Theban Mountains, your feet would
stumble over the bones of departed generations. Princes, priests, and
warriors, after reposing thousands of years in their deep seclusion, are
dragged forth by poor peasants, and scattered around the doors of
those
cavern-like excavations in the everlasting hills.

Lighting a torch or candle, you may wander along the rock-walled
galleries several hundred feet into the heart of the summits, on each
side of which are the apartments of death.

Inscriptions, three thousand years old, can be distinctly traced.

How little thought the Hebrews, while toiling under the shadow of
palaces, or flying at night from the mighty realm of Egypt, of what we
find to-day along the banks of the Nile!

The doom of Babylon, with that of the great invaders and conquerors of
Palestine, is equally wonderful and instructive.

Probably no nation of antiquity was more distinguished for luxury and
corrupt pleasures than this unrivalled city.

Its last king, Nabonnidus, reigned about one hundred years before
Christ
appeared; and in less than that time afterward, the city walls enclosed
a hunting ground or park for the recreation of Persian monarchs. We
cannot well imagine a more complete destruction than has overtaken
the
once rich and gay metropolis. The ruins are a number of mounds,
formed
of crumbled buildings, and strewn all over with pieces of brick,
bitumen, and potter's vessels.

The Assyrian kings of western Asia, also invaded the Holy Land. They ruled a vast and powerful realm, whose principal city was Nineveh, to which Jonah was sent with a message from God.

Sennacherib, the monarch who reigned seven hundred years before Christ,
marched his armies against the cities of Judah and took them. Not satisfied with the terms of surrender he threatened further invasion.

At this crisis, in answer to prayer, Jehovah sent his angel to destroy the troops; and in one night the unseen messenger of destruction slew one hundred and eighty-five thousand men.

Of this miraculous defeat a gifted but irreligious and unhappy poet has sung:

    And there lay the steed with his nostrils all wide,
    But through them there rolled not the breath of his pride;
    And the foam of his gasping lay white on the turf,
    And cold as the spray of the rock-beaten surf.

    And there lay the rider, distorted and pale,
    With the dew on his brow and the rust on his mail;
    And the tents were all silent, and the banners alone,
    And the lances unlifted, the trumpets unblown.

    And the widows of Ashur are loud in their wail,
    And the idols are broke in the temple of Baal;
    And the might of the Gentiles, unsmote by the sword,
    Hath melted like snow at the glance of the Lord.

Now the greater part of the country which once formed Assyria, is under
the sway of the Turks.

Mosul, a missionary station of the American Board of Foreign Missions, is believed to mark the site of ancient Nineveh.

The original inhabitants of Assyria, in modern history, are the Kurds; a barbarous and warlike race. Some of these live in villages, and others roam over the country. They are said to resemble, in personal appearance, the Highlanders of Scotland.

But the most remarkable fact in regard to the population, is the ancient church of the Nestorians, among the mountains. This Christian people have for ages maintained their independence, defying the storms of revolution that have swept over all the country around their mountain home.

Dr. Grant, a missionary, thinks they are descendants of the "lost tribes of Israel." We recollect to have seen in the hands of the venerable missionary, Rev. Dr. Perkins, a copy of the Scriptures preserved for many hundred years by them: sometimes hidden away, to prevent its destruction by its enemies.

Not long ago, one of the Nestorian bishops, Mar Yohanah, visited this country, and attracted much attention. A Jew-like, noble man personally,
and a devout Christian.

But if you look on the map of Asia, you will see that Mosul and the Nestorian country is in Persia, and may wonder what it has to do with Assyria. In the conquests which weakened and divided the Assyrian empire, new kingdoms were formed; and while none can now accurately
trace the boundaries of that great monarchy, we have the later outline of Persia. More will be said of this remarkable kingdom when we come to
the story of Mordecai and Esther.

The thrones of these ancient monarchies were, at first, no more than an ornamented arm-chair, higher than ordinary seats, with a footstool for the royal feet. Then it was made in more massive form and richly carved,
with steps ascending to it.

Some of the thrones were of ivory, adorned with gold; and it is recorded, that Archelaus addressed the multitude from a throne of solid gold--a magnificent fortune in itself. Thus gradually the throne became the highest symbol of power, and is often applied to Jehovah's sovereignty. He is represented as sitting upon a throne of light, and around him continually, attending angels, veiling their faces with their wings, and waiting to hear and obey his mandates; crying with their voices of celestial music, "Holy, holy, holy, Lord God Almighty, which was and is, and is to come!" A "crystal sea" is before this "White Throne" of a pure and just authority, and on it worships a resplendent host. Every sound and sight of glory and honor, that language can express, or the finest imagination picture, is ascribed to that eternal royalty.

Next to the throne, the crown became a sign of authority, although it was applied, at first, to other ornaments for the head, properly called coronets, garlands, tiaras, bands, mitres, etc.

The idea of a kingly crown was suggested by the diadem, which was a fillet--a mere band like that used to bind the long hair worn by the people--but richer and of a different color. It was natural and easy, with the increase of power and wealth, to make the crown a more costly and showy symbol of kingly sway.

David wore a crown of gold set with jewels, he took from the king of the
Ammonites.

The more modern crowns of Asia, where all the kings reigned, of whom we
have read in these pages, are of different shapes, and some of them very rich and expensive, ornamented with precious stones and plumes of the rarest kind.

Crowns are also often mentioned in the Bible as an emblem of power; and
the Christian conqueror of his sins and the world, it is written, shall have "a crown of life."

The sceptre was the third token of sovereignty. The word originally signified a staff of wood of the length of a man's height. Later, it was smaller in form, and often plated with gold, and enriched with various decorations. Inclining, or holding out the sceptre was a mark of royal favor; and kissing it by another, a sign of submission.

Jehovah's rule is mentioned frequently in the inspired record, under this figure. "His sceptre is a right sceptre," in one of the declarations, which even the wicked and most wretched on account of transgression, dare not deny.

Under its wide dominion are Heaven, Earth, and Hell, not only, but a universe whose boundaries neither man nor angel can ever reach.

"He is God over all, and blessed forever!"

How amazing the truth of such a king and kingdom! Under the unsleeping
eye of the Sovereign, the planet wheels on its axis with startling velocity, and the insect creeps on the grain of sand. A Russian poet beautifully sung:

Oh, thou Eternal One! whose presence bright,
  All space doth occupy, all motion guide!
Unchanged through time's all devastating flight,
  Thou only God, there is no God beside!

Being above all beings! mighty one,
  Whom none can comprehend, and none explore!
Who filled existence with thyself alone;
  Embracing all, supporting, ruling o'er!
  Being, whom we call God, and know no more!

Thou art! directing, guiding all. Thou art!
  Direct my understanding then to thee;
Control my spirit, guide my wandering heart,
  Though but an atom 'mid immensity.
Still I am something fashioned by thy hand!
  I hold a middle rank 'twixt heaven and earth,
On the last verge of mortal being stand,
  Close to the realms where angels have their birth,
  Just on the boundaries of the spirit land.

Oh, thoughts ineffable! Oh, visions blest!
  Though worthless our conceptions all of thee;
Yet shall thy shadowed image fill our breasts,
  And waft its homage to thy Deity.
God! thus alone my lowly thoughts can soar;
  Thus seek thy presence--Being wise and good!
'Midst thy best works admire, obey, adore!

And when the tongue is eloquent no more,
The soul shall speak in tears of gratitude.

Ascent of Elijah.

Elisha on His Death Bed.

THE BIBLE AND THE HOLY LAND

PATRIARCHS, KINGS, AND KINGDOMS.

HEBREW CAPTIVES; OR, MORDECAI AND ESTHER.


The next pictured scene is in the Court of Persia. It will not be forgotten that Daniel was a captive in Babylon under the last kings, and probably died there after the city was taken by Cyrus. Of this great man's history as a captive we shall learn more when we go with the prophets of God in their peculiar mission.

Nabonadrius, the son of Darius, usurped the throne after his father's death; and after reigning several years, Cyrus, a nephew of Darius, a Persian general who was occupied in foreign wars, turned his attention to the reigning monarch.

He marched against the gorgeous metropolis, and besieged it for two years in vain. He at last thought of a stratagem which displayed his genius and boldness of action. He determined to turn the channel of the Euphrates, which went through the whole length of the city, from the walls where it entered, and get into the capital through the dry channel, under the massive pile which no battering rams could crumble.
He succeeded in making a new bed for the stream, and his troops went into Babylon over a path washed for ages by the waters of the Euphrates.

Media, a word some suppose to be derived from Madai, the son of Japheth,
was the name of a region adjacent to ancient Assyria, inhabited by warlike hordes for centuries. The little that is said of these people in the Bible, is in connection with the Persians. Both seemed to have become one nation; first the Medes gaining the ascendancy, and then the
Persians. But the darkness which rests upon the origin of the Asiatic lands bewilders the most careful historian.

The conspicuous appearance of the Medes and Persians begins with Cyrus the Great, the conqueror of Babylon, a remarkable monarch in power, glory, and character.

The picture of the magi who journeyed from the east to find the infant Messiah, presents a peculiar view of the Persians and Arabians. Among these gentile nations were men of great attainments in whatever of philosophy and astrology there was in the world. The Ethiopian race is represented, and it may have been that dark faces were over the wonderful child. Color was evidently then no honor or disgrace; the man
was the object of regard or scorn. More will be said of these wonderful travellers in the more appropriate place in the annals of Palestine. Cyrus the first, and noble Persian monarch, was kindly disposed to-ward
the captive Jews, and Daniel had great influence over him. In the very year of his conquest he issued a decree, in which, after acknowledging the supremacy of the Lord, and that to him he owed all kingdoms, he gave
full permission to the Jews in any part of his dominions, to return to their own land and to rebuild the city and temple of Jerusalem. No sooner were the favorable dispositions of the king thus made known, than
the members of the latter captivity--those of the tribes of Judah, Benjamin, and Levi--repaired in large numbers to Babylon from their different places of residence; some to make preparations for their journey; and others, who had no intention to return themselves, to assist those who had. Most of the existing race had been born in Babylonia, and in the course of years families had established themselves in the country, and formed connections, and gathered around
them comforts which were not easily abandoned. Only a minority availed
themselves of the decree in their favor; the most of the people choosing to remain in the land of their exile; and it has always been the opinion of the Jews that the more illustrious portion of their nation remained in Babylonia.

The first return caravan was organized and directed by Zerubbabel, the grandson of king Jehoiachim, and by Jeshua, a grandson of the last high-priest Jozadak. The number of persons who joined them was about fifty thousand, including above seven thousand male and female serv-

ants.
Before they departed, Cyrus restored to them the more valuable of the sacred utensils, which had been removed by Nebuchadnezzar, and preserved
by his successors, and which were now to be again employed in the service of the sanctuary. Zerubbabel was also entrusted with large contributions toward the expense of rebuilding the temple, from the Jews
who chose to remain behind. The beasts of burden in this caravan exceeded eight thousand. In the book of Ezra, the names of the families which returned to this first colony, and in those which followed, are carefully given.

The incidents of the journey are not related. On reaching Palestine the caravan repaired at once to Jerusalem, which they found utterly ruined and desolate. Before they separated to seek habitations for themselves, they raised a large sum by voluntary contributions toward the rebuild-ing
of the temple. Then they employed themselves in securing dwellings and
necessaries for their families; and at the ensuing Feast of Tabernacles again repaired to Jerusalem, where sacrifices were offered on an altar erected upon the ruins of the temple. After this the people applied themselves zealously to the necessary preparation for the restoration of that edifice. In a year from the departure from Babylon, the preparations were sufficiently advanced to allow the work to be commenced; and, accordingly, the foundations of the second temple were
then laid with great rejoicings and songs of thanksgiving. While the work proceeded, the Samaritans manifested a desire to assist in the work, and to claim a community of worship in the new temple. This was
declined by the Jews on the ground that the decree of the Persian king extended only to the race of Israel.

The Magi offering Presents.

Being thus frustrated in their design, the Samaritans employed every means they could devise to thwart the undertaking. Their origin appears
to have given them considerable influence at the Persian court; and although they could not act openly against the plain decree of Cyrus, an unscrupulous use of their money and influence among the officers of the
government enabled them to raise such obstructions, that the people were
much discouraged, and the work proceeded but languidly, and at length
was suspended altogether. From this lethargy they were roused by the exhortations and reproaches of the prophet Haggai; and the building was
resumed with fresh zeal.

The new temple was dedicated with great solemnity and joy. The Jews were

allowed the free exercise of their religion and laws, and the government was directed by a governor of their own nation, or by the high-priest, when there was no other governor. There was, in fact, a distinct commonwealth, with its own peculiar institutions; and, although responsible to the Persian king, and to his deputy the governor-general of Syria, it was more secure under the protection of the monarch than it would have been in complete independence. The dreadful lesson taught by
the desolation of the land, the destruction of the temple, and the captivity of the people, had effectually cured the Jews of that tendency to idolatry which had been their ruin. But, as time went on, the distortion of character which had been restrained in one direction broke forth in another; and although they no longer went formally astray from
a religion which did not suit their depravity, they, by many vain and mischievous fancies, fabricated a religion suited to their dispositions out of the ritual to which they adhered.

Early in the reign of Artaxerxes, son of the mighty Xerxes, the Hebrews went to work on the beloved city with a regular plan of its rebuilding, including an encircling wall.

This king had learned by reading and traditions, the veneration which his most distinguished predecessors had shown for the God of Israel; and
about seven years after he ascended the throne, he commissioned Ezra, the priest and scribe, to take charge of the religious service at Jerusalem. And he was, in reality, the governor or viceroy under the monarch.

Those of the Hebrews who desired to do so, were invited to return with him, and others who remained, were to pay contributions for the use of the temple.

To this fund the king himself and his council contributed large sums of money; and the ministers of the royal realms west of the Euphrates, were
enjoined to furnish Ezra with silver, wheat, wine, oil, and salt, that the sacrifices and offerings of the temple should be constantly kept up; all of which is said to have been done in order to avert from the king and his sons, the wrath of the God of the Hebrews, who was held in

much
honor at the Persian court.

An exemption from all taxes was also promised to persons engaged in
the
service of the temple; but this boon did not induce any of the Levitical
tribe to join the caravan which assembled on the banks of the river
Ahava, in Babylonia: and it was with some difficulty that Ezra at last
induced some of the priestly families to go with him. The whole caravan
was composed of one thousand seven hundred and fifty-four adult
males--making, with wives and children, about six thousand persons.
As a
party thus composed had little military strength, and as the journey
across the desert was then, as it always has been, dangerous from the
Arab tribes by which it is infested, they felt considerable anxiety on
this account. But Ezra, from having said much to the king of the power
of God to protect and deliver those that trusted in him, felt
disinclined to apply for a guard of soldiers; and thought it better that
the party should, in a solemn act of fasting and prayer, cast themselves
upon the care of their God. Their confidence was rewarded by the perfect
safety with which their journey was accomplished. In four months they
arrived at Jerusalem.

While Ezra, with his sealed commission from Artaxcrxcs, was urging on
the noble work at Jerusalem, an unexpected danger to his people in
Babylon and its provinces arose--a sudden and fearful crisis in destiny.

Among the captives there was Esther, a Hebrew maiden. The Persian
king,
to commemorate his victorious and prosperous reign, extending from
Judea
to Ethiopia, and embracing a hundred and twenty-seven provinces,
made a
magnificent feast, which continued six months. This was to display his
power and wealth, before the nobility of his realm, and representatives
from the conquered provinces of his spreading empire. At the expira-
tion
of this brilliant entertainment, he gave the common people, without
distinction, a feast of seven days in the court of his palace. The rich

canopy and gorgeous curtains, with their fastenings--the tall columns,
the golden couches, and tesselated floors--are described as "white,
green, and blue hangings, fastened with cords of fine linen and purple
to silver rings, and pillars of marble: the beds were of gold and
silver, upon a pavement of red, and blue, and black, and white marble."

Our Saviour Teaching in the Temple.

Of this grandeur, in the ashes strewn by wasting ages, are imposing
remains. Modern travellers pause before "the vast, solitary, mutilated
columns of the magnificent colonnades," where youth and beauty
graced
the harems of Persian monarchs.

Upon this occasion, the queen had a private pavilion for her female
guests. But during the successive days of dissipation, the mirth waxed
loud in the apartments of the king. The flashing goblet circulated
freely, and his brain became wild with "wine and wassail." As the
crowning display of his glory, Vashti, in her jeweled robes and diadem,
must grace the banquet. The command was issued, and the messenger

sent.

This mandate, requiring what at any time was contrary to custom, the
appearance of a woman, unveiled, in an assemblage of men, now when
revelry and riot betrayed the royal intoxication, overwhelmed the
queen
with surprise. A thousand wondering and beaming eyes were upon her
during the brief pause before answering the summons. Her proud re-
fusal
to appear, roused the fury of Ahashuerus, already mad with excite-
ment.
It would not answer to pass by the indignity, for a hundred and
twenty-seven provinces were represented at his court, and the news of
his sullied honor would reach every dwelling in his realm, and curl the
lip of the serf with scorn. The nobles fanned the flame of his
indignation. Unless a withering rebuke were administered, their
authority as husbands would be gone, and the caprice of woman make
every
family a scene of daily revolution.

Vashti was divorced--and to provide for the emergency, his courtiers
suggested that he should collect in his harem all the beautiful virgins
of the land, and choose him a wife. Among these was Hadassah, the
adopted daughter of Mordecai. He urged her to enter her name among
the
rivals for kingly favor. It was not ambition merely that moved Mordecai.
He had been meditating upon the unfolding providence of God toward
his
scattered nation, and felt that there was deeper meaning in passing
events than the pleasures and anger of his sovereign. Arrayed richly as
circumstances would permit, the beautiful Jewess, concealing her
lineage, joined the youthful procession that entered the audience
chamber of Ahashuerus, where he sat in state, to look along the rank of
female beauty, floating like a vision before him.

The character of Esther is here exhibited at the outset; for when she
went into the presence of the king, for his inspection, instead of
asking for gifts as allowed by him, and as the others did, she took only
what the chamberlain gave her. Of exquisite form and faultless features,
her rare beauty at once captivated the king, and he made her his wife.

Mordecai was a man of a noble heart, grand intellect, and unwavering integrity; there was nevertheless an air of severity about him--a haughty, unbending spirit; which with his high sense of honor and scorn
of meanness would prompt him to lead an isolated life. We have some-times
thought that even he had not been able to resist the fascinations of his young and beautiful cousin, and that the effort to conceal his feelings had given a greater severity to his manner than he naturally possessed. Too noble, however, to sacrifice such a beautiful being by uniting her fate with his own, when a throne was offered her; or perceiving that the lovely and gentle being he had seen ripen into faultless womanhood could
never return his love--indeed, could cherish no feeling but that of a fond daughter, he crushed by his strong will his fruitless passion. In no other way can I account for the life he led, lingering forever around the palace gates, where now and then he might get a glimpse of her who
had been the light of his soul, the one bright bird which had cheered his exile's home. That home he wished no longer to see, and day after day he took his old station at the gates of Shushan, and looked upon the magnificent walls that divided him from all that had made life desirable. It seems also as if some latent fear that Haman, the favorite of the king--younger than his master, and of vast ambition, might attempt to exert too great an influence over his cousin, must have prompted him to treat the latter with disrespect, and refuse him that homage which was his due. No reason is given for the hostility he manifested, and which he must have known would end in his own destruction.

Whenever Haman, with his retinue, came from the palace, all paid him the
reverence due to the king's favorite but Mordecai, who sat like a statue, not even turning his head to notice him. He acted like one tired of life, and at length succeeded in arousing the deadly hostility of the haughty minister. The latter, however, scorning to be revenged on one man, and he a person of low birth, persuaded the king to decree the slaughter of all the Jews in his realm. The news fell like a thunderbolt on Mordecai. Sullen, proud, and indifferent to his own fate, he had defied his enemy to do his worst; but such a savage vengeance had never

entered his mind, It was too late, however, to regret his behavior. Right or wrong, he had been the cause of the bloody sentence, and he roused himself to avert the awful catastrophe. With rent garments, and sackcloth on his head, he travelled the city with a loud and bitter cry, and his voice rang even over the walls of the palace, in tones that startled its slumbering inmates.

Humility Exemplified--Giving Alms in Secret.

It was told Esther, and she ordered garments to be given him, but he refused to receive them, and sent back a copy of the king's decree, respecting the massacre of the Jews, and bade her go in and supplicate him to remit the sentence. She replied that it was certain death to enter the king's presence unbidden, unless he chose to hold out his sceptre; and that for a whole month he had not requested to see her. Her
stern cousin, however, unmoved by the danger to herself, and thinking only of his people, replied haughtily that she might do as she chose; if she preferred to save herself, delivery would come to the Jews from

some
other quarter, but she should die.

From this moment the character of Esther unfolds itself. It was only a passing weakness that prompted her to put in a word for her own life, and she at once rose to the dignity of a martyr. The blood of the proud and heroic Mordecai flowed in her veins, and she said: "Go, tell my cousin to assemble all the Jews in Shushan, and fast three days and three nights, neither eating nor drinking; I and my maidens will do the same, and on the third day I will go before the king, and if I perish, I perish!" Noble and brave heart! death--a violent death--is terrible; but thou art equal.

There, in that magnificent apartment, filled with perfume, and where the
softened light, stealing through the gorgeous windows by day, and shed
from golden lamps by night on marble columns and golden-colored couches, makes a scene of enchantment, behold Esther, with her royal apparel thrown aside, kneeling on the tesselated floor. There she has been two days and nights, neither eating nor drinking, while hunger, and
thirst, and mental agony have made fearful inroads on her beauty. Her cheeks are sunken and haggard--her large and lustrous eyes dim with weeping, and her lips parched and dry, yet ever moving in inward prayer.
Mental and physical suffering have crushed her young heart within her, and now the hour of her destiny is approaching. Ah! who can tell the desperate effort it required to prepare for that terrible interview.
Never before did it become her to look so fascinating as then; and removing with tremulous anxiety the traces of her suffering, she decked herself in the most becoming apparel she could select. Her long black tresses were never before so carefully braided over her polished forehead, and never before did she put forth such an effort to enhance every charm, and make her beauty irresistible to the king.

At length, fully arrayed and looking more like a goddess dropped from the clouds, than a being of clay, she stole tremblingly toward the king's chamber. Stopping a moment at the threshold to swallow down the
choking sensation that almost suffocated her, and to gather her failing

strength, she passed slowly into the room, while her maidens stood
breathless without, listening, and waiting with the intensest anxiety
the issue. Hearing a slight rustling, the king, with a sudden frown,
looked up to see who was so sick of life as to dare to come unbidden in
his presence, and lo! Esther stood speechless before him. Her long
fastings and watchings had taken the color from her cheeks, but had
given a greater transparency in its place, and as she stood, half
shrinking, with the shadow of profound melancholy on her pallid, but
indescribably beautiful countenance, her pencilled brow slightly
contracted in the intensity of her excitement, her long lashes dripping
in tears, and lips trembling with agitation; she was, though silent, in
herself an appeal that a heart of stone could not resist. The monarch
gazed long and silently on her, as she stood waiting her doom. Shall she
die? No; the golden sceptre slowly rises and points to her. The
beautiful intruder is welcome, and sinks like a snow wreath at his feet.
Never before did the monarch gaze on such transcendent loveliness;
and
spell-bound and conquered by it, he said, in a gentle voice: "What wilt
thou, Queen Esther? What is thy request? It shall be granted thee, even
to the half of my kingdom!"

Woman-like, she did not wish to risk the influence she had suddenly
gained, by asking the destruction of his favorite, and the reversion of
his unalterable decree, and so she prayed only that he and Haman
might
banquet with her the next day. She had thrown her fetters over him,
and
was determined to fascinate him still more deeply before she ventured
on
so bold a movement. At the banquet he again asked her what she desired,
for he well knew that it was no ordinary matter that had induced her to
peril her life by entering unbidden his presence. She invited him to a
second feast, and at that to a third. But the night previous to the
last, the king could not sleep, and after tossing awhile on his troubled
couch, he called for the record of the court, and there found that
Mordecai had a short time before informed him through the queen, of
an
attempt to assassinate him, and no reward been bestowed. The next
day,
therefore, he made Haman perform the humiliating office of leading his

enemy in triumph through the streets, proclaiming before him: "This is
the man whom the king delighteth to honor." As he passed by the gallows
he had the day before erected for that very man, a shudder crept
through
his frame, and the first omen of coming evil cast its shadow on his
spirit.

Herod's Cruel Massacre.

The way was now clear to Esther, and so the next day, at the banquet,
as
the king repeated his former offer, she, reclining on the couch, her
chiseled form and ravishing beauty inflaming the ardent monarch with
love and desire, said in pleading accents: "I ask, O king, for my life,
and that of my people. If we had all been sold as bondmen and bond-
women,
I had held my tongue, great as the evil would have been to thee." The
king started, as if stung by an adder, and with a brow dark as wrath,
and a voice that sent Haman to his feet, exclaimed: "Thy life! my queen?
Who is he? where is he that dare even harbor such a thought in his
heart? He who strikes at thy life, radiant creature, plants his

presumptuous blow on his monarch's bosom." "That man," said the lovely
pleader, "is the wicked Haman." Darting one look of vengeance on the
petrified favorite, he strode forth into the garden to control his
boiling passions. Haman saw at once that his only hope now was in moving
the sympathies of the queen in his behalf; and approaching her, he began
to plead most piteously for his life. In his agony he fell on the couch
where she lay, and while in this position the king returned. "What!" he
exclaimed, "will he violate the queen here in my own palace!" Nothing
more was said; no order was given. The look and voice of terrible wrath
in which this was said, were sufficient. The attendants simply spread a
cloth over Haman's face, and not a word was spoken. Those who came in,
when they saw the covered countenance, knew the import. It was the
sentence of death. The vaulting favorite himself dare not remove it--he
must die, and the quicker the agony is over, the better. In a few hours
he was swinging on the gallows he had erected for Mordecai.

After this, the queen's power was supreme--every thing she asked was
granted. To please her he let his palace flow in the blood of five
hundred of his subjects, whom the Jews slew in self-defence. For her he
hung Haman's ten sons on the gallows where the father had suffered
before them. For her he made Mordecai prime minister, and lavished
boundless favors on the hitherto oppressed Hebrews. And right worthy was
she of all he did for her. Lovely in character as she was in person, her
sudden elevation did not make her vain, nor her power haughty. The same
gentle, pure, and noble creature when queen, as when living in the lowly
habitation of her cousin, generous, disinterested, and ready to die for
others, she is one of the loveliest characters furnished in the annals
of history.

It is a little singular that the words, God or Providence, are not
mentioned in the whole book of Esther. The writer seems studiously to
have avoided any reference to them, as if he did not wish to recognize
the interposition of Heaven in any of the events that transpired; while
his narrative is evidently designed to teach nothing else. The hand of

Providence is everywhere seen managing the whole scheme.

But the greatest acts of Providence awaken the least attention among
blind, mortal men. We are startled when some great occurrence meets
us,
but overlook the vast effects which follow causes that attracted no eye
but God's. We see the flying timbers and flaming ruins of a
conflagration, and forget that a concealed spark did it all.

A noble mind and body are wrecked, and many weep; yet how few
think that
the blast of moral ruin which stranded the life-bark, was once the quiet
breath of a mother's unholy influence leading the boy astray.

So the splendid career of a hero and patriot, like Mordecai, Moses, or
Washington, is less glorious than the simple decision made amid the
conflicting emotions of youthful aspiration to honor God and serve a
struggling country.

Jehovah illustrates this principle in all his administration. What to
Elijah on the solemn mount was the sweep of the hurricane, rending the
cliffs and tossing rocks like withered leaves in air--the thunder of the
earthquake's march--the blinding glow of the mantling flame--
compared to
the "still small voice" that thrilled on his ear, so full of God! It is
not strange that there is to be a reckoning for "idle words" even, for
they have shaken the world, and their echo will never die away.

Their mutual love and devout character, remind us of the affectionate
fidelity to each other and to God, of Ruth the Moabitess, and her Hebrew
mother-in-law Naomi, who lived in the time of the Judges.

Naomi's family were self-exiled on account of famine in Palestine. Ruth
had married a man of Moab; but he and her father-in-law died. A sister
whose husband was brother to her own, was also a widow; and when
Naomi
determined to return to her native land, at her request, Orphah sought
her people and friends.

Ruth would not leave the pilgrim to the Holy Land. Embracing Naomi,

she
said: "Entreat me not to leave thee, for where thou goest I will go, and
where thou lodgest, I will lodge: thy people shall be mine, and thy God
my God: where thou diest I will die, and there will I be buried: naught
but death shall part us."

Beautiful and brave heart! home, and friends, and wealth, nay, the gods
she had been taught to worship, were all forgotten in the warmth of her
affection. Tearful yet firm, "Entreat me not to leave thee," she said.
"I care not for the future; I can bear the worst; and when thou art
taken from me, I will linger around thy grave till I die, and then the
stranger shall lay me by thy side!" What could Naomi do but fold the
beautiful being to her bosom and be silent, except as tears gave
utterance to her emotions. Such a heart outweighs the treasures of the
world, and such absorbing love, truth, and virtue, make all the
accomplishments of life appear worthless in comparison.

God blessed their devotion to him and each other, giving his special
tokens of favor to the young heroine from Moab. Upon reaching Bethlehem,
she went into the fields of a kinsman of her mother-in-law, Boaz, a
wealthy citizen, to glean after the reapers. He inquired after her,
became interested in her, and, remembering his obligations on account
of
their relationship, married her. An honorable portion and plenty
crowned
the homeless wanderings of Ruth and Naomi, as they did the captivity
of
Mordecai and Esther.

About two hundred years after the death of the latter, the Hebrew
Scriptures were translated into Greek by the order of Ptolemy
Philadelphus, the Egyptian sovereign of Palestine, making the famous
Septuagint--the name probably referring to seventy-two persons en-
gaged
on the work.

A little over two centuries passed, and the Roman armies began their
conquests in Asia. Less than a score of years later Herod the Great
governed Judea, under the Roman emperor. This Herod, whose reign
closed

the ancient annals of Palestine, was an Edomite--a cruel and ambitious
man.

Less than thirty years passed, and one of the darkest, bloodiest acts of
any sovereign since time began, disgraced the reign of Herod.

Jerusalem was astonished by the arrival of three sages from the distant
east, inquiring for a new-born king, saying that they had seen "his
star," and had come to offer him their gifts and homage. They found
him
in the manger at Bethlehem: and then repaired to their own country
without returning to Jerusalem, as Herod had desired. The jealousy of
that tyrant had been awakened by their inquiry for the "King of the
Jews;" and as their neglect to return prevented him from distinguishing
the object of their homage, he had the inconceivable barbarity to order
that all the children in Bethlehem under two years of age should be put
to death, trusting that the intended victim would fall in the general
slaughter; but Joseph had previously been warned in a dream to take
his
wife and the infant to the land of Egypt, whence they did not return
till after the death of Herod.

That event was not long delayed. In the sixty-ninth year of his age.
Herod fell ill of the disease which occasioned his death. That disease
was in his bowels, and not only put him to the most cruel tortures, but
rendered him altogether loathsome to himself and others. The natural
ferocity of his temper could not be tamed by such experience. Knowing
that the nation would little regret his death, he ordered the persons of
chief note to be confined in a tower, and all of them to be slain when
his own death took place, that there might be cause for weeping in
Jerusalem. This savage order was not executed. After a reign of
thirty-seven years, Herod died In the seventieth year of his age.

Sir Walter Scott's beautiful "Hebrew Hymn" will fittingly close these
sketches of Palestine:

  When Israel, of the Lord beloved,
    Out from the land of bondage came,
  Her father's God before her moved,
    An awful guide, in smoke and flame.
  By day along the astonished lands,

The cloudy pillar glided slow;
By night Arabia's crimsoned sands
  Returned the fiery columns' glow.

There rose the choral hymn of praise,
  And trump and timbrel answered keen;
And Zion's daughters poured their lays,
  With priests' and warriors' voice between.
No portents now our foes amaze,
  Forsaken Israel wanders lone;
Our fathers would not know Thy ways,
  And Thou has left them to their own.

But present still, though now unseen,
  When brightly shines the prosperous day,
Be thoughts of Thee, a cloudy screen,
  To temper the deceitful ray.
And oh! when stoops on Judah's path,
  In shade and storm, the frequent night,
Be Thou long-suffering, slow to wrath,
  A burning and a shining light.

Our harps we left by Babel's streams,
  The tyrant's jest, the Gentile's scorn,
No censer round our altar beams,
  And mute our timbrel, trump, and horn,
But thou hast said, "The blood of goat,
  The flesh of rams I will not prize,
A contrite heart, an humble thought,
  Are more accepted sacrifice."